God's Words Bring *Life*

Christ's Life becoming Your Life

B. Lee McDowell

GOD'S WORDS BRING LIFE
Copyright © 2019 by B. Lee McDowell
Published by Dowadad Press
   A division of Lee McDowell Christian Ministries, Inc.
   P.O. Box 633244, Nacogdoches, TX 75963
   leemccm.wixsite.com/lmcm

ISBN # 978-0-9980359-1-8

All rights reserved. No part of this publication may be reproduced, stored in a retrieval system, or transmitted in any form or by any means – electronic, mechanical, photocopy, recording, or any other – without the prior written permission of the publisher. The only exception is brief quotations in printed reviews.

All scripture quotations are taken from the King James Version of the Bible
Cover design and photo by Rick West
Printed in the United States of America

*I dedicate this book to
all the wonderful Believers who are
wandering through the wilderness of the
religious, legalistic life they have been taught
and led to believe is Christianity.*

*Christ is Christianity.
We are Believers in Christ.
As Christians, we are placed IN Christ.
As Christians, Christ is ALIVE IN us.
The Life of Christ is Christianity
in every Believer, wanting to Live
each day in our earthsuit…
before removing our earthsuit and
giving us our new Heavenly suit
to live the rest of Eternity with Him.*

*May the Christians who read these pages come
to know and enjoy our Lord Jesus Christ
as their LIFE NOW and FOREVER!*

Acknowledgements

I remember thinking one day about 3 months after being Born Again of just how many Christians I was meeting that did not seem to know *who they were in Christ*. It was almost unbelievable to me. Our Pastor, John Morgan (Sagemont Church, Houston, Texas) was always preaching on the incredible aspects of Believers being *in Christ*.

Ever since beginning to discover what the Apostle Paul was telling the church at Ephesus of our inheritance as children of God, I began a search for the fundamental, foundational Truths that can undergird our Life as a Christian. All throughout the New Testament are beautiful, uplifting words that have brought Life to my life. It is with this idea, and my gathering notes over the years, that I want to share what God has done for His children.

I thank our Lord for His plan. I thank Him for His clear teaching giving us the benefits that are ours as a part of the family of God. And I thank Him for His clear teaching giving us the benefits of the indwelling Holy Spirit in each Believer. Wow! And as my friend Tom Hagen is constantly saying, "Thank You, Jesus!"

It is with a very grateful heart that I acknowledge the many wonderful pastors, evangelists, teachers, missionaries, and friends who have brought so much of God's Word to my attention and to my benefit. Their encouragement to dig a little deeper, do more meditating, and to search the original languages behind our English translation have given me the desire to not just *know* God, but to have a vibrant *experience* of God.

All of this has led me to find the multitude of Truth that *God's Words Bring Life,* His Life becoming my Life.

I am grateful for my friend, Rick West, who loves God and His Truths. Rick is also a lover of photography. His eye, his ingenuity, and his camera brought the cover photo to reality. Barbara and I also get to minister with Rick and his wife, Abby, at Festival Park in downtown Nacogdoches every Sunday morning…Christ In The Park.

Lee McDowell Christian Ministries

B. Lee McDowell, Author

there is nothing the presence of Christ cannot overcome

All books by B. Lee McDowell are available in Nacogdoches, and online @ Amazon/Kindle preaching or teaching engagements are calendared on *love offering* basis

eGroups (via email) to study books in depth

to sign up for eGroups or LMCM Mailing List, contact us…

1737 CR 2051 Nacogdoches, TX 75965

Phone: 936-559-5696   email: leemccm@gmail.com

blog: www.leemccmviews.blogspot.com

website: www.leemccm.wixsite.com/lmcm

author's page: www.amazon.com/-/e/B083LQXJZ4

Table of Contents

	Foreword		9
	Preface		11
	Introduction		13
1	2 Timothy 3:14-17	The Holy Scriptures	15
2	John 6:63	What Is A LIFE Verse?	17
3	Genesis 3:1	Questioning God's Word	20
4	Matthew 13:10-11	Parabolic Teaching	22
5	John 3:7	The New Birth	27
6	1 John 5:12	Saved & Sure	29
7	2 Corinthians 5:17	A New Creation	32
8	1 Thessalonians 5:23	Trichotomy of Mankind	35
9	1 Corinthians 2:16	Mind of Christ	43
10	Proverbs 1:5	Wise Beyond Your Years	47
11	Proverbs 4:23	The Battle Is For Which Mind	50
12	Matthew 13:11	It Is A Privilege To Be Able To Understand	52
13	Acts 16:31	What Is It To Believe?	56
14	John 1:12	Believe And Receive	60
15	Hebrews 11:1	Do We Know What Faith Really Is?	63
16	Hebrews 11:6	Faith Is Everything With God	66
17	Galatians 2:20	It's Not My Faith; It's Christ's Faith I Live By	68
18	Romans 10:17	Christ's Faith Comes By Our Hearing	70
19	Proverbs 3:5-6	Trust Is The Turning Point	73
20	John 5:39-40	The Man of The Holy Scriptures Brings Life, Not the Words	75
21	Colossians 3:4	Christ's LIFE Is My Life	77
22	John 10:10	Christ's LIFE More Abundantly	79
23	John 15:5	Branches On The Vine	83
24	Ephesians 1:3	In Christ	85
25	Colossians 1:27	Christ In Us	89

26	Colossians 1:19; 2:9-10	Complete In Christ	93
27	Ephesians 3:17-19	The Fullness of God	96
28	Romans 4:4	The Principle of Grace	99
29	Ephesians 4:24	The Practice of Grace	102
30	Romans 12:1-2	Abandoned To God	107
31	Romans 8:11	Holy Spirit Power Alive In Us	111
32	Ephesians 3:20-21`	Exceeding Abundantly	114
33	Philippians 4:13	Do All Things	117
34	Ephesians 1:3	Blessed With All Spiritual Blessings	120
35	Galatians 5:22-23	Fruit of Holy Spirit	123
36	2 Timothy 1:7	Holy Spirit of Power, of Love, and of Sound Mind	126
37	John 10:11	The Good Shepherd and His Sheep	128
38	Psalm 23:1	The Work of Our Good Shepherd	131
39	John 8:32,36	Truth (Christ) Makes Us Free	133
40	John 14:27	The Peace of Christ	135
41	Isaiah 26:3	What Is It To Have Christ's Peace? And How?	138
42	Philippians 4:11	Learning To BE Content	141
43	Psalm 119:165	Never Be Offended	144
44	Proverbs 12:25	NO Depression EVER	146
45	Philippians 4:19	Our Divine Supply	149
46	2 Timothy 2:1-2	From Faith To Faith	154
47	Luke 16:10	Faithful In the Least	156
48	2 Peter 3:18	Grow In Grace	158
49	Proverbs 1:7	The Fear of the LORD	162
50	Philippians 2:13	His Work…His Will	166
51	Romans 8:28	All Things Working Together	169
52	Philippians 1:6	God Will Complete What He Started	171
	Scriptural References		174
	On Being Born Again		178
	Books by B. Lee McDowell		180
	About the Author		182

Foreword by Barbara McDowell

Not growing up reading the Bible, I was introduced to the Word of God the day I heard the words "ye must be Born Again." Two days later I trusted Jesus Christ as my Savior and was Born Again. My introduction to the Bible started a new awareness of God's Word being alive to me. Each time a new Bible verse was preached or read, I would think, "WOW, that's incredible!"

Over the last almost 40 years I have read the Bible through from front to back several times and over the years God has given me special verses that are living to me. They comfort me, encourage me and remind me of God's presence in my life. Gods Words bring Life to me.

This book is about 52 of these Life verses that are important to me and Lee. They have been studied and their true meaning revealed. This same process can be applied to any favorite verse. There are certainly many more meaningful verses. I've memorized several so that they are available to meditate on and speak to God about without having a Bible. I hope you will realize this important opportunity you have…to have personal Life verses that guide you through Life as a Christian.

Read this book and start your own list of favorite verses that have helped you. Take each verse, get some study helps and let God open His treasures to you.

Preface

This book, like all I will write, has taken 40 years to become reality. It began back in May, 1980, when my wife Barbara and I were Born Again in Pastor John Morgan's office at Sagemont Church, Houston, Texas. Having visited Sagemont two days earlier and hearing Bro. John preach on *Ye Must Be Born Again,* John ch.3, vs.1-7, we had made an appointment to find out more about how to be *Born Again*.

Ever since that day, God has had us on a journey to find more of His Truth to be *made free* from the bondage of erroneous teaching we had been given the previous 30+ years. What you will find in this book are things I have been reading, making notes, asking questions, living, writing, organizing, and finally compiling into this written work.

God's TRUTH does MAKE us FREE. That is, His Truth that we believe and receive. Too many folks hear or read Truth, but don't believe or receive Him. They may be Christians (Believers), but they are Unbelieving Believers on too many things of God.

God's Words Bring Life is a compilation of 52 writings about what I call *Life Verses*. Each one brings the Life of Christ to our Life (Him) in us to be Lived out of our earthsuit. IF you want His Life, and MORE of His Life, read each chapter with His Eyes, His Ears, His Mind, and His Heart looking for Truth that will bring His Life to you in abundance and His Joy throughout your being!

This book is about Spirit, Truth, and Life.

Introduction

God's Words Bring Life shows how the Word of God can come alive off the pages of the Bible with *Christ's Life Becoming Your Life*. What more could a Christian truthfully want!

I want you to read each word anticipating God to show Himself strong in YOUR Life each and every day. Each chapter will give one more picture of just Who Christ wants to be in your earthsuit.

The early foundational chapters will show where *His Life* comes to us, and then we begin to build how to *experience Him*. Keep in mind one premise as you read: there is nothing the presence of Christ cannot overcome…or bring. It is the very Truth of the *presence* of God in each Believer that makes Christianity what it is. Without Him *inside*, no one is a Christian. God says so. Discover this and you will be carried forward knowing that every step you take, every place you are, HE is with you.

Early on you will discover the picture of what a Born Again Saint *looks like* as a New Born Believer now created in the image of God that Adam and Eve were created with. When you *see* it, you will never walk with God the same as before.

In the middle, you will see much of *who you are IN Christ* and *Who Christ is IN you!* When I first began to learn of all I am IN Christ 40 years ago, I just about flipped out! And then, I was raised to a whole different realm when I began to learn all about Who Christ is IN me. Wow! I would love to be sitting with you when you get to those chapters…

When you get to the end, you will be filled with the fullness of God. You will have Him as your Life. HE will be *living* and *doing* all that you were created in Him to be and do, knowing that He will complete what He started at your New Birth and continuing until He takes you home.

So, to get started, we begin with the foundation of all foundations, the *Word of God, the Holy Scriptures*. Enjoy the read!

BLM

God's Words Bring *Life*

Chapter 1

The Holy Scriptures

> But continue thou in the things which thou hast learned and hast been assured of, knowing of whom thou hast learned them; And that from a child thou hast known the holy scriptures, which are able to make thee wise unto salvation through faith which is in Christ Jesus. All scripture is given by inspiration of God, and is profitable for doctrine, for reproof, for correction, for instruction in righteousness: That the man of God may be perfect, thoroughly furnished unto all good works.
> 2 Timothy 3:14-17

I cannot think of anything of this earth that is more precious than to hold in my hands the Word of God. The Inspired, Inerrant, Infallible Word of God. The Holy Scriptures. Before you go any further in this book, take a few moments to soak on this.

Now listen. Truth is so narrow that even the slightest deviance is falsehood. And God has said it is *Truth* that *makes us free*. I want to be free from all falsehood, free from all error, free from all lies (of which God has also told us our enemy is the *father of all lies*). *God's Truth, Jesus, the Word,* makes us free.

So, let us get back to the heart of this beginning chapter. Little needs to be expounded upon for you to get what I want for you to start with. Just cherish that with the Holy Scriptures, and the Mind of Christ within you, you can be given revelation from God into the vast riches of His Truth.

The Holy Scriptures. They are just that. *Holy Scriptures. Ta Hiera Grammata.* The authoritative writings which are The Word of God. Paul told Timothy it is they which are *able to make thee wise unto salvation through faith which is in Christ Jesus.* And then Paul goes further to make certain we know that these authoritative writings come from the *inspiration of God* and are for our profit, our gain, for *doctrine, reproof, correction, and instruction in righteousness.*

Finally, Paul told Timothy (and us) that *the man of God* (the Greek here for *man* is *anthropos,* a generic name of the species without any respect to sex, man or woman) *may be perfect* (the Greek here for *perfect* is *artios,* complete) *thoroughly furnished unto all good works.*

Now, listen, I learned a long time ago (1980) that *The Holy Scriptures* are the writings for Life for us. Years later it became real to me that they are Christ's Life in us, for us. It is my prayer that for any question in life that you have you will turn to *The Holy Scriptures* for God's answers, God's directives, and God's ways. Actually, you will learn later in this book that *The Holy Scriptures* are to take you TO God, for He is Truth and He is Life, not just words on a page.

Heavenly Father, thank You that You have preserved Your inspired, inerrant, and infallible Word for us to be led to You through our reading and to be able to grasp Truth, You, in all we read. May You grow us in Your Grace through our searching of the Holy Scriptures.

And Holy God makes you perfect, complete!

Chapter 2

What Is A LIFE Verse?

*It is the Spirit that quickeneth; the flesh profiteth nothing:
the words that I speak unto you, they are spirit, and they are life.
John 6:63*

More Life-giving and Life-changing words have never been spoken. Jesus told us clearly and distinctly of His Life, His Spirit, and the power, provision, and promise of every Word to come from Him.

Two things to know right up front: 1) this book is about 52 *Life Verses* I listed and now expound upon for your benefit (they have benefitted me immensely over the years), 2) each verse is Truth that leads us TO Christ (Who IS Truth, and He is THE Life that brings LIFE to us) for all He will do for you, and not just some empty words.

John 6:63 is my theme verse for what I call *Life Verses*, verses where the Lord speaks to the Spiritual Heart in Believers and reveals some of His Life to us. It is important for us to know and understand the Spiritual implications His Words and His Life have for us.

Let's notice some great things He mentions in this verse: "It is the Spirit that quickeneth." First, it is a capital S, noting Holy Spirit. Second, it is He Who *quickeneths*. This is a Greek word, *zoopoieo*, to make alive, vivify. Most often this is used when speaking of salvation, but at all times it gives the meaning of the words having Life, His Life. Now notice Jesus says that "the flesh profiteth nothing." *Flesh* here and in many instances in the NT speaks NOT of the bodily flesh, but that *residue* of what is left of the *old man* in the *old soul* (see ch.8 & trichotomy diagrams) in Believers. The Greek word is *sarx*, best understood as that part of a Believer *under any controlling influence other than Christ*. The *old* mind, emotions, and will working *naturally* in opposition to Christ form the *flesh, sarx*.

Then Jesus makes it very specifically plain and clear that HIS WORDS are Spirit, and they are Life (I like to capitalize anything that is a part of Christ). Now we all know that the words in what is called a Red-letter Edition of a Bible are words the authors of each book are quoting of Jesus' actual words spoken around 33-36 A.D. However, God tells us that EVERY word, even the jots and tittles, of the ENTIRE Holy Scriptures are His Words (2 Timothy 3:16, "All Scripture is given by inspiration" – God-breathed – of God). Therefore, each and every word of God's Word stands as bringing Spirit and Life to Believers who have the capacity to grasp them as such (see ch.4).

So, let's think about this for just a moment. We have THE Word of God. As Believers we have Christ's Soul to *read, hear, and understand* His Word and receive what He tells us in a Supernatural way. Unbelievers do not have this capacity, and cannot receive, understand, or comprehend what we can.

> But the natural man receiveth not the things of the Spirit of God: for they are foolishness unto him: neither can he know them, because they are spiritually discerned. 1 Corinthians 2:14

What a privilege to hold the Holy Scriptures as a Believer, and be able to read and grasp what Almighty God is saying to each and every one of us…these Truths can be our great treasure!

There is one thing we must stop and mention at this point. Revelation is where God reveals what He says to us in a special way at special moments in our life. Sometimes we read a verse, and it doesn't mean much to us. Another time, another time, another time, many times…and then WHAM! It hits us like a brick…WOW! I *hear* or *see* something from God that I have not seen before.

THEN is when that verse becomes a *Life Verse* particularly for YOU! Hallelujah!

OK, we start this book of so-called *Life Verses* I have received from God to pass on to you, knowing that the first time you read them they will mean a little something, or perhaps not much. But as you continue over your life to read, and re-read, these writings, some day Holy Spirit will *zoopoieo* His Words in you and THAT MOMENT will have come.

That verse will have a special place in your Spiritual Heart (remember, when I capitalize some word that otherwise might not be capitalized, it is because I want you to know I am speaking of a part of Christ in you, not just an ordinary part!). BUT, REMEMBER…THESE VERSES ARE TO TELL US OF CHRIST AND TAKE US TO HIM.

This book will only cover what I have felt led of God to include for now…52 text verses. There will be many more verses mentioned in the book, but 52 that will be the focus of each different writing. For your convenience and easy access, I have included a chronological list of all Scriptural verses in the manuscript, with references showing each time a verse is located in the manuscript. I find such info extremely helpful for reference and study.

This is a book that gives you some of my most memorable learnings, and then things I have shared in many ways over the years God has given to me for His ministry. I did not want all that He gave me to NOT be put in writing for others, especially my kids and grandkids, to have for whatever reason. Every Believer is to be equipped and minister as God opens the doors. Well, amen!

Oh, wait! I hope you will actually take the time to read ALL of John chapter 6. Part of John 6 clearly enunciates and delineates God's *plan of salvation* (see *On Being Born Again* at the end of this book). The first few verses are about Jesus feeding the 5,000, a widely-known story. And then vs. 28-29 are the text for another writing in this book. It would be wise and fruitful for you to stop before you go on and read the entire chapter (which makes me think of another important thought: have the Holy Scriptures with you, if at all possible, each time you open the pages of this book…THAT will prove wise and fruitful also!).

Dear Jesus, thank You for making Your Words Spirit and Life. May we realize our great need for Your Life in our earthsuit. Teach us in every *Life Verse* in this book just what Your Life will bring to us and work through us.

And LIFE always quickeneths!

Chapter 3

Questioning God's Word

> Now the serpent was more subtle than any beast
> of the field which the LORD GOD had made.
> And he said unto the woman, Yea hath God said...?
> Genesis 3:1

Asking questions about God's Word is totally different than questioning God's Word. It is very important to know the difference.

Trillions of times since this moment in the Garden of Eden has the devil come calling and challenging anything and everything that God has said and done. It is his soul - his *natural mind, natural emotions, natural will, and natural heart* to do so. Fallen/lost man has the devil's soul and thinks the same way. Christians living out of the *residue* that remains in us are just as capable of doing so.

Now, listen. It is never wrong to ask *relevant questions* about *What do the Holy Scriptures/God say about* _____? Nor is it wrong to ask *Why?* of the Holy Scriptures/God when seeking an *honest answer*. BUT, it is never OK to question whether the Holy Scriptures/God are correct in saying anything. Or, to question in a challenging or disregarding way of anything the Holy Scriptures/God have said. (or, to challenge/disregard anything God has done).

IF Believers would ever *see* and acknowledge that questions of this latter sort are truthfully questioning or attacking God, they may stop short of going there.

I remember my first Sunday School teacher, Louis Cole, at Sagemont Church, Houston, Texas, 1980, after I was Born Again. I could hardly spell B-I-B-L-E, much less know anything it said. Louis was an excellent teacher. Knowing very little about the Truths of Scripture and God, I had several questions when Louis was teaching. Louis would teach something. I would ask a question. Louis would give God's explanation. I would be blessed.

Class would be over and one of the guys would come up and say, "I'm sure glad you asked that question. I've been wanting to ask that, but never felt comfortable about doing so. Thank you." I would think as the guy walked away – *Why wouldn't anyone ask any question of a teacher/preacher to get an answer that would grow our knowledge of God, God's Truth, and God's ways?*

Listen! Never hesitate to ask a question to find out *what* God has said, has done, or is doing. Never *question* God's Word (whose Mind is around a 1,000,000,000,000,000+ and counting IQ).

Omniscient God, may we always take You at Your Word, and only seek to know more of it and more of You.

Chapter 4

Parabolic Teaching

And the disciples came, and said unto Him (Jesus),
Why speakest Thou unto them in parables?
He answered and said unto them,
Because it is given unto you to know the mysteries
of the kingdom of heaven, but to them it is not given.
Matthew 13:10-11

This is one of the most dramatic teachings in all of Scripture. Telling us about Jesus teaching in parables, *and WHY*. Parabolic teaching. Make sure you get what this is all about. It will change so much of your understanding of the Holy Scriptures. Jesus went on to say to His disciples,

> For whosoever hath, to him shall be given, and he shall have more abundance: but whosoever hath not, from him shall be taken away even that he hath. Therefore I speak unto them in parables: because they seeing see not; and hearing they hear not, neither do they understand. And in them is fulfilled the prophecy of Isaiah, which saith, By hearing ye shall hear, and shall not understand; and seeing ye shall see, and shall not perceive: For this people's heart is waxed gross, and their ears are dull of hearing, and their eyes they have closed; lest at any time they should see with their eyes, and hear with their ears, and should understand with their heart, and should be converted, and I should heal them. But blessed are your eyes, for they see: and your ears, for they hear. For verily, I say unto you, That many prophets and righteous men have desired to see those things which ye see, and have not seen them; and to hear those things which ye hear, and have not heard them. Matt. 13:12-17

I never will forget the first time I read these verses in Matthew 13. I was floored! Jesus telling His disciples that He is speaking to the masses in a way that they will not understand. The Spiritual implications of this are staggering, far past this one parable of Jesus recorded in Matthew 13. Listen to what Matthew 13:34-35 tell us…

> All these things spake Jesus unto the multitude in parables; and without a parable spake He not unto them: That it might be fulfilled which was spoken by the prophet, saying, I will open my mouth in parables; I will utter things which have been kept secret from the foundation of the world.

My, oh my, oh my. Matthew records that Jesus spoke ONLY in parables to the multitudes, knowing they would not be able to understand and grasp what He was truthfully telling them. This had been prophesied years before (Psalm 78:2 speaks of such). I Corinthians 2:7, Ephesians 3:9, and Colossians 1:26 speak of this type of *revealing* of the mysteries of old. The *revealing* is for God's children only!

Matthew is not the only writer to record this incident and the specifics of Jesus teaching in parables. It is important to mention some particular verses in Mark chapter 4.

> And He began again to teach by the seaside: and there was gathered unto Him a great multitude, so that He entered into a ship, and sat in the sea; and the whole multitude was by the sea on the land. And He taught them many things by parables, and said unto them His doctrine. 4:1-2

> And He said unto them, He that hath ears to hear, let him hear. And when He was alone, they that were with Him with the twelve asked of Him the parable. And He said unto them, Unto you it is given to know the mystery of the kingdom of God: but unto them that are without, all these things are done in parables: That seeing they may see, and not perceive: and hearing they may hear, and not understand; lest at any time they should be converted, and their sins should be forgiven them. vs.9-12

And with many such parables spake He the word unto them, as they were able to hear it. But without a parable spake He not unto them: and when they were alone, He expounded all things to His disciples. vs. 33-34.

Mark gives us one detail that is extremely worth noting: v.34, *and when they were alone, He expounded all things to His disciples*. The disciples with Jesus at this moment needed Him to *expound/explain* the parable to them. Relax a moment and I will explain why, when according to Jesus' words just prior He says the mysteries were to be known by them.

So many Believers have either never been taught this next Truth, or it doesn't seem to be that important to them. But I tell you it is crucial to understanding the actions and words of the disciples following Jesus prior to the moment recorded in Acts 2:1-4, the giving of Holy Spirit (and actually a *filling* at this first giving) to the Believers gathered in the upper room of the place several disciples abode (Acts 1:13).

Here is the monumental Truth: prior to God giving ALL Believers Holy Spirit to indwell our earthsuits, the disciples walking with Jesus on earth were seeing things with the *natural eyes* just like an Unbeliever. They were hearing things with the *natural ears* just like an Unbeliever. They were thinking and understanding everything with the *natural mind* just like an Unbeliever. Jesus had to expound and give them more explanation in order for them to grasp the Spiritual Truth *behind* Jesus' words.

In essence, He had to open their *natural* to receive His *supernatural*, prior to their being given the Supernatural Holy Spirit. Only after Holy Spirit brought Christ's Supernatural Eyes and Ears and Mind could the Saints See, Hear, and Comprehend the Supernatural Truths. WOW!

Now, hold on! Every Believer today has two minds. One is the *natural* we were given at our physical birth. The second is the *Supernatural Spiritual* we were given at our Spiritual birth. Believers can either see, hear, and think with the *natural* still in us from our physical birth, or we can *See, Hear, and Think* with the *Supernatural Spiritual* we were given when Born Again. Wow. Wow. Wow.

Therefore, we can *read* the Holy Scriptures and *get* what God is telling us in the *Spiritual Mind*, OR we can read the Holy Scriptures and miss what God is telling us…just as if we were still Unbelievers in the *natural mind*.

Now let me get back to what I want you to know about *parabolic teaching* right now. Teaching in parables can be in different manifestations. A common one is the use of an earthly picture/story that has the hidden Heavenly meaning. Another is the giving of instructions for people to do given things that can only be done completely and acceptably to God BY the Lord Jesus Christ. My friend, Michael Wells always used to say, "Teaching that lands at my feet and tells me something I must do is false teaching. Teaching that lands at Jesus' feet and tells me what He will do for me is Truth." All the lists of *to do* are things (all are Spiritual things) that should be manifested through our earthsuit, BUT by Holy Spirit and not *us (our flesh)*.

I agree with Michael completely, however let me say I think that the *false teaching* Michael speaks of can be more easily grasped if seen as *parabolic teaching*. God telling us something that is Truthfully only that which Jesus can do 100% of the time, 100% acceptable to God. WHY are those *instructions, rules, commands, and laws* which the *natural* cannot *do acceptably to God* given then? So the *natural* will come to the end of himself, and turn to God as his only hope. *Parabolic teaching* is necessary for God to get some Unbelievers to give up trying *to do* (including *earning their way to Heaven*), and *trust God* for whatever need they have.

This is not as difficult or complicated as it may seem. In fact, Christians for years and years have been saying, "The Holy Scriptures are God's Love letter to His kids." Well, if that is so (and it is), how would a person not in the family of God expect to See, Hear, or Understand God's Love letter to His kids? Have you ever written a love letter to someone? Would you expect someone who doesn't know you, or know your loved one, to read your letter and understand the *hidden things* in your letter? No.

One final thing. Some Scripture is historical, some scientific, some mathematical, some musical. These can be known and understood with the *natural mind*. It is the *Spiritual* that is *parabolic*. That is why the world will argue that Scripture contradicts itself, or is full of untruths, or "how can _____?" How? *Parabolic*.

Believers are to know of the *parabolic teaching*, recognize it with the *Supernatural Spiritual Mind*, and not be concerned with any debate or disbelief by anyone living in the *natural mind* (be it an Unbeliever or a Believer living in the *lesser mind*).

> But the Comforter, which is the Holy Ghost, whom the Father will send in my name, he shall teach you all things, and bring all things to your remembrance, whatsoever I have said unto you. John 14:26

Oh GOD, how can we ever be thankful enough to have been given Supernatural Holy Spirit to be us in this earthsuit so that we can See, Hear, Grasp, and Understand Your Heavenly Truths. Teach us all of Your mysteries You want us to have.

The Lord has given Supernatural Spiritual Truths to be known only by the Supernatural Spiritual us. Well, amen.

Chapter 5

The New Birth

Marvel not that I said unto thee, Ye must be born again.
John 3:7

My wife, Barbara, and I were Born Again on May 20, 1980. We trusted in and received Lord Jesus Christ as our personal Savior in Pastor John Morgan's office, Sagemont Church, Houston, Texas, during an appointment with him to discuss further what we had heard him preach on Sunday, the 18th. Believing, trusting, and receiving Truth from the Word of God results in biblical faith. We began the process of receiving Christ when we first heard the preaching of the Word of God that Sunday morning. Going to church is one thing. Going to church (or a bible study, or any so-called Spiritual meeting) where the Word of God is truthfully read and expounded upon is a whole different matter.

Let me give you the text of Pastor Morgan's message that day…

> There was a man of the Pharisees, named Nicodemus, a ruler of the Jews: The same came to Jesus by night, and said unto Him, Rabbi, we know that thou art a teacher come from God: for no man can do these miracles that Thou doest, except God be with him. Jesus answered and said unto him, Verily, Verily, I say unto thee, Except a man be born again, he cannot see the kingdom of God. Nicodemus saith unto Him, How can a man be born when he is old? can he enter the second time into his mother's womb, and be born? Jesus answered, Verily, verily, I say unto thee, Except a man be born of water and of the Spirit, he cannot enter into the kingdom of God. That which is born of the flesh is flesh; and that which is born of the Spirit is spirit. Marvel not that I said unto thee, Ye must be born again. John 3:1-7

This is the story of a very respected leader of the Jews in that day and his coming to Jesus at night to inquire more about spiritual matters. However, Jesus turned the meeting into a Gospel presentation in His first words to Nicodemus. And in the process, Jesus compared our physical birth with this Spiritual birth. I use a capital S because this is not just any old *spiritual* birth!

Peter in his 1st epistle emphasized this same comparison,
> Being born again, not of corruptible seed, but of incorruptible, by the word of God, which liveth and abideth for ever. 1 Peter 1:23

And then in his second epistle, Peter makes an even greater declaration,
> According as His divine power hath given unto us all things that pertain unto life and godliness, through the knowledge of Him that hath called us to glory and virtue: Whereby are given unto us exceeding great and precious promises: that by these ye might be partakers of the divine nature, having escaped the corruption that is in the world through lust. 2 Peter 1:3-4

I would prefer all the things that pertain to God be capitalized so that the Source and importance could be easily seen when reading the Scriptures. Anyway, by our hearing, believing, trusting, and receiving the Word of God (Romans 10:8-17) and likewise the same with the record God gave of His Son (ref. 1 John 5:10-12, 13), God confirmed our believing and trusting to the point of His creating/giving us the New Birth. It is the Word of God creating His Life in our earthsuit to be *our* Life.

Now listen, the New Birth gives us Christ's Life via Holy Spirit indwelling us. His Divine Nature. Think of ALL we have been given as Peter tells us in those two magnificent verses at the start of his second epistle!

And the Supernatural Spiritual New Birth is the greatest moment of anyone's life!

Chapter 6

Saved and Sure

He that hath the Son hath life:
and he that hath not the Son of God hath not life.
1 John 5:12

Very few aspects of Life as a Christian truly compare with a *Know-So Salvation*. What do I mean by those words? Simply this: that it is so important to *KNOW* that we have truthfully been Born Again. That translates into confidence, comfort, and complete assurance and peace.

1 John 5:12 is one of those many verses that I wish the King James translators had capitalized any word that signified the personification or manifestation of God Himself. Just as the name Son with a capital S shows clearly who is being mentioned, *life* should have a capital L to show clearly that God's Word is speaking about Christ's Life here.

He that hath the Son hath Christ's Life would do wonders for us as we read the Holy Scriptures. First, it would be a constant emphasizing of His Life being ours, His Life being so important in the overall picture. Second, it would differentiate between His Life being what we received at our New Birth and the life we received at our physical birth, or just life in general. Third, with all that awareness, we could more easily be convinced of our salvation.

Is it important to God that His Saints *KNOW* they are Born Again? YES! Look at what John wrote (remember, ALL Scripture is from God even though individual Saints were the penmen) in the verse that follows our chapter's text:

> These things have I written unto you that believe on the name of the Son of God; that ye may know that ye have eternal life, and that ye may believe on the name of the Son of God. 1 John 5:13

What? *KNOW*. And the Greek for *know* is *eidos*, *to perceive with the mind* (and Paul had to be speaking of the Mind of Christ within Saints), *understand, know intuitively* as contrasted with *ginosko* which means to know experientially. We can *eidos*. We can *KNOW*. Our Spirit is Holy Spirit. He speaks to our Christ-Heart. We have the Mind of Christ to *eidos* what someone who is not a Christian cannot *eidos*, for they do not have the Mind of Christ…only the *natural mind* all humans are physically born with.

Here is something very interesting. To have the Son of God is to have Holy Spirit. He, Holy Spirit is God indwelling us. He is Life itself, Eternal Life (always has been, always will be). Do you realize that Holy Spirit in us links us to Forever (always been, always will be)?

And look at this…Romans 8:9, 16:
> But ye are not in the flesh, but in the Spirit, if so be that the Spirit of God dwell in you. Now if any man have not the Spirit of Christ, he is none of his. v.9
> The Spirit itself beareth witness with our spirit, that we are the children of God. v.16

Wow! Total equation of Holy Spirit and Jesus Christ and God, and our connection in Him.

Now listen, no wonder John closes verse 12 in 1 John by saying that *he that hath not the Son of God hath not life*. What God is speaking of is His Life. Eternal Life.

So, do you see why I consider this to be a *Life Verse?* I can tell you from almost 40 years of experience in ministry that many – way too many – Saints do not have the confidence, comfort, and complete assurance and peace of their salvation. A real tragedy.

Let me show you another place in Scripture that can be of great help in *knowing* you are a Child of God, Saved and Sure…2 Peter 1:5-11:
> And beside this, giving all diligence, add to your faith virtue; and to virtue, knowledge; And to knowledge, temperance; and to temperance, patience; and to patience, godliness; And to godliness, brotherly kindness; and to brotherly kindness, charity. For if these things be in you, and abound, they make you that ye shall neither be barren nor unfruitful in the knowledge of our Lord Jesus Christ. But he that lacketh these things is

> blind, and cannot see afar off, and hath forgotten that he was purged from his old sins. Wherefore the rather, brethren, give diligence to make sure your calling and election sure: for if ye do these things, ye shall never fall: For so an entrance shall be ministered unto you abundantly into the everlasting kingdom of our Lord and Savior Jesus Christ.

Wow! Words that show us *how* we can be certain we are Saints, words that show us *how* so many are uncertain of their salvation (doubters…forgetters that they have been purged of old sins), and words that tell us about an *abundant* entrance into the everlasting kingdom! Well, amen.

Aside from the fact that I just slipped in several great *Life Verses* in addition to the chapter text, let me encourage you to notice God mentioned twice what we are to be diligent about, and…He gave us a ministry to fellow Saints that might be doubting their salvation. I have used these very verses numerous times in showing Saints what is causing their doubting. (Only Saints will ever doubt whether they are Saved. The lost, *natural* mind cannot think of that.)

Being Saved and Sure frees a Believer to move on in their Life as a Christian.

Chapter 7

A New Creation

Therefore if any man be in Christ, he is a new creature:
old things are passed away;
behold, all things are become new.
2 Corinthians 5:17

This is one of the most profound statements in all the Bible. God tells of a *new creation* which only He is capable of creating! God, only, can create. Man makes. Creation is bringing something into being which has never before been. God does that. Man takes two or more *somethings* and *makes* something different, but cannot *create* something new that has never existed in and of itself.

Every Christian is a new *being* which has never before *been*. This is a Truth that so many Believers, preachers, and teachers either do not recognize or basically ignore. A Christian is not a *do-over* or *restoration*. A Christian is not a *renovation*. A Christian is not a *refurbishing*. A Christian is brand new, a new entity that did not exist in any shape, form or fashion before. And the way most handle this creation is a cause of so much misunderstanding and misinformation which leads to so much confusion and ignorance like giving Believers a *list* of do's and don'ts to become a *good* Christian, with some thinking that is how one *becomes* a Christian. Every Christian is a *perfection* of God's *creating*, and needs no improvement or becoming *good* or *better*. That is the fallacy of so much preaching and teaching today.

What did God say about His *creation* in Genesis 1:31?

    And God saw every thing that He had made, and behold,
    it was very good…

Aha. *Very good*. All *creation* by God He called simply *good* or *very good*. So, why does anyone today think that this *new creation* by God needs improvement, or to prove to be *good?* Is it because there is something in every Christian that is *not so good?* Yes, there is. But, it is not a part of the *new creation*. It is a part of the remnant (*residue*) the Apostle Paul spoke of in Romans (particularly in chapters 6, 7, & 8). And, a huge question arises at this point: is it possible to *improve* the *sin* that is in our members? No.

> But I see another law in my members, warring against the law of my mind, and bringing me into captivity to the law of sin which is in my members. Romans 7:23

So...all the efforts by Christian preachers and teachers to tell us that we need to *improve* the sin *residue* are useless. All the efforts by Christians to try and *improve* the sin *residue* are useless. So, is there an *answer* or *solution* to this so-called *dilemma?* Yes.

> O wretched man that I am! who shall deliver me from the body of this death? I thank God through Jesus Christ our Lord. So then with the mind I myself serve the law of God; but with the flesh the law of sin. Romans 7:24-25

The solution is to abandon *self* to God and let Holy Spirit Live His LIFE through us. There is *no other way*. Working to improve *flesh* is useless, a waste of effort...it cannot be done. Live in the Soul of Christ *and see the law of God served!*

Enjoy being a *new creation*. Get any thoughts off the *residue*. One way to start is to learn all you can about what this *new creation* gives us. Knowing *who you are IN CHRIST* (Ephesians ch.1 for starters) and Who *Christ is IN US* (Colossians 1:27 for starters) are both great beginning points of getting an understanding of all that God intended for us as *new creations.* (see ch.24 and ch.25 to begin to get information from the Word of God about both of these).

Before we go any further, notice in our text verse that God speaks of being *in Christ* as relative to our being a *new creature/new creation*. And then He says two important things that need to be fully and accurately understood. Incorrect interpretation has led many to false ideas and faulty efforts, even to failing to continue believing they have been Born Again (becoming this *new creation*). Let me set the record straight:

- *old things are passed away* – when there is a *therefore* there, we need to see why it is there. The three preceding verses (vs. 14-16) tell us we are not to look at the *flesh* (earthsuit) and its activity when we consider *living* (or anyone else's *living*). We are not to live unto ourselves but unto Him Who died for us. These are Spiritual admonitions, not for or of the flesh. The *old life* (of demonic spirit – opposition to God) is no longer. Crucified. Removed. *Passed away.*

- *behold, all things are become new* – we are a *new Life* that is Spiritual, of Christ's Spirit and Soul. That is what is *new*. Any other consideration is a false consideration. Holy Spirit immediately indwells every Believer. Christ's Mind, Emotions, Will, and Heart immediately indwell every Believer. These combine to become the Believer's *new Life*.

Now listen, too many well-intentioned Believers (including preachers and bible teachers) say something like this: "I thought Bill (or Jim, or Sally) got Saved, but they still drink (or smoke, or cuss)."

All flesh. Nothing Spiritual, EXCEPT they are making a point of *old flesh* not passing away and *new flesh* not looking like they think it should *as being the tell-tale sign of this person not being a New Creation*. False theology. False interpretation of 2 Corinthians 5:17 (totally out of context with the verses before and after).

So, we must get our theology lined up with Scripture. We need to get excited about being a *new Creation* IN CHRIST with CHRIST (Holy Spirit) IN US! This *Creation* in us is *very good*.

And God's Creations are always very good!

Chapter 8

Trichotomy of Mankind

*And the very God of peace sanctify you wholly;
and I pray God your whole spirit and soul and body
be preserved blameless unto the coming of our Lord Jesus Christ.*
1 Thessalonians 5:23

This could be one of the most important chapters you read in this book. It will be of little impact IF you just read it, and don't own it.

When someone speaks of *man* we must immediately ask the question: "What *man* are you talking about?" If they say, *a male*, or possibly the generic reference to the *species* of humans differentiated from animals, then we can possibly have an honest discussion about that *man*. However, if they say, "You know, *man*...all humans." At that point we cannot possibly have an honest discussion. There is no *man* in general, and there hasn't been since the *fall* of Adam & Eve. Since that moment in history, *man* (male and female human beings) became *lost man* (cursed, unregenerate, an Unbeliever, *natural man*, *old man*...among other descriptions in the Holy Scriptures). All males and females since the *fall* have been physically born as such. Actually, Adam & Eve, as created in the *image of God* in the Garden in their innocence, can be identified with a diagram of their trichotomy in that state.

When God imputed righteousness to Adam & Eve, and to multitudes of others in Old Testament days, these became *Saved man* (regenerated, Believers, child of God...among other descriptions in the Holy Scriptures). Since the crucifixion, resurrection, and ultimate return to Heaven of our Lord Jesus Christ, all individuals who have trusted Him for salvation have been imparted righteousness from God. All males and females since their New Birth are Supernaturally Spiritually different than before.

Therefore, any look at a diagram of *man* needs to include diagrams of *lost man* and of *Born Again man*. Any talk about *man* must include a recognition of WHICH *man* we are talking about. As for this book, unless I specifically mention *lost man*, I will be talking about *Born Again man*. I have included three diagrams with some important points listed that give us needed information for adequate information on both *persons*. And I use *Born Again man* as my preferred designation for Christians. *Saved* can mean many things to many people. *Born Again* is specifically Christian.

The term *trichotomy* is a word that speaks of 3 parts, classes, or categories, etc. of whatever is being described. *Tri* means three. *Chotomy* means a subdivision of parts of a whole. The number three (3) is important in God's vocabulary. It is most often interpreted as referring to *God's sovereignty*. One of the physical aspects of God's control in human lives is this *trichotomy of His Creation of man…Adam & Eve*. These first two humans were created with three distinctive *parts* – spirit, soul, and body. To my knowledge, no one has ever drawn a diagram using the three circles to show the *trichotomy* of Adam & Eve in their created state. Even though I have such a diagram, it will have to wait for another book. Here we are looking for the *trichotomy of lost man* and the *trichotomy of Born Again man*. These three diagrams will go a long way in showing us just exactly *who* each is, and *how* each lives. Knowing all that I show in the three diagrams gives us a distinct advantage in understanding why there is such a battle going on between Christians and non-Christians, and IN individual Christians themselves. This battle is Spiritual. This battle is the basis of all conflict in all Christians, even though 99.9% *see* and *fight* in a physical realm instead of a Spiritual realm. Therefore, so many conflicts are misunderstood, mistaken, and really cannot be solved. At least not in the realm they are fought. Listen, a fight between *good* and *evil* in the *natural mind* can never be *won*!

Are you ready to SEE *who you used to be* and *who you are now*?

Simple Diagrams of "Images"

LOST MAN ~ UNBELIEVER ~ SINNER

BORN AGAIN MAN ~ BELIEVER ~ SAINT

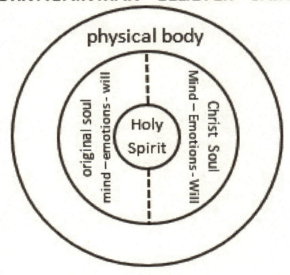

UNBELIEVER
Not a Christian
(called Lost man, Sinner, Unforgiven sinner, Unregenerated man)

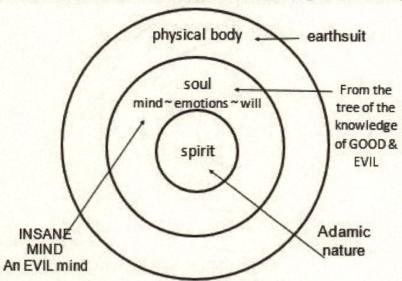

This diagram pictures the "Adamic nature" of Unbelievers since the Fall, that which all are physically born with. ALL humans are physically born with this spiritual nature (spirit) and soul. Notice both are with a "small" letter, indicating the absence of Holy Spirit and Christ's Soul.

UNBELIEVER
humanism (man is god)
pride (me, not Christ)
self-righteousness
complexity
unbelief
distrust
lies

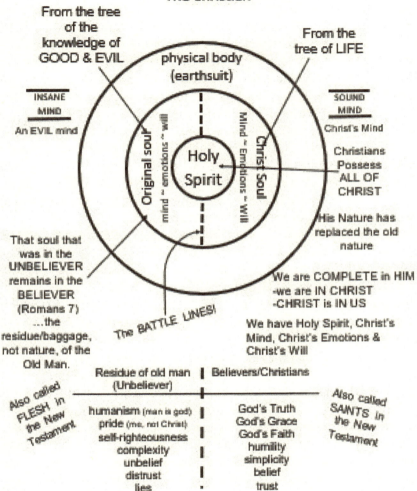

The first diagram shows the most simple pictures of the three parts (trichotomy) of *lost man* and *Born Again man.* This is to give a clear diagram of the *spirit, soul, and body (earthsuit)* of each.

The second diagram gives a detailed picture of *lost man* with his Adamic nature (life) and unregenerate soul (mind, emotions, will). What most do not realize is that his state is that of being totally without God, capable of the most insane, evil thoughts-feelings-actions the enemy can conjure up. It should never shock us when a *lost man* does some of the most evil things we see him do. It is the demonic personified.

The third diagram pictures the *Christ Nature* (Life) of all Born Again Believers/Christians/Saints. WOW! What an incredible NEW MAN. The CHILD of GOD. And, every Christian has Christ's Soul (Christ's Mind, Christ's Emotions, Christ's Will, Christ's Heart).

Now, one more thing that is very important, but really no way to *diagram:* the *Heart.* Hopefully my explanation will convey what God is wanting us to know, but yet so few actually do.

The *Heart* is the summation of the activity of the Christ *Soul.* The *Soul,* remember, houses the *Mind, Emotions, and Will* of Christ. (likewise, with small letters, there is a *heart* the same for the unregenerated, *lost soul*…which remains in the Believer, left side of diagram).

When the Apostle Paul gave us the context and process by which *Christ's Faith* becomes *Our Faith,* he spoke of *hearing* and *believing.* We see this in Romans 10:9-10,

> That if thou shalt confess with thy mouth the Lord Jesus, and shalt believe in thine heart that God hath raised Him from the dead, thou shalt be saved. For with the heart man believeth unto righteousness; and with the mouth confession is made unto salvation.

Pisteuo en sou kardia. Looking at the trichotomy diagrams we see when the Holy Scriptures speak of the *Heart,* they are speaking of the interaction of the components of the *Soul (Christ's Mind, Christ's Emotions, Christ's Will).* This verifies that to *believe/pisteuo* involves more than just the mind, a mental assent.

So, take your time to look over the diagrams. Familiarize yourselves with each, particularly with all the information attached to the particular circles, as well as the information in general. Everything is important.

Everything points us to what we need to understand about *each man*, and to be able to interact with each and with ourselves.

To not leave you hanging about the *trichotomy of Adam & Eve*, I am working on a book of at least seven (7) *trichotomy* diagrams that will give a lot of needed information to better grasp God's overall revelation in Scripture about Himself *(in* Heaven*)*, Christ on earth, and even Christians (and Christ) in Heaven.

What do you think of these three diagrams? Really something, aren't they? Let me remind you that the information on these three diagrams are important Truths to know. And they will help you to know much about things going on in your lives, as well as the lives of family and friends and everyone you have any interaction with. I will discuss this at great length later on, but interaction between Christians (you) and non-Christians can be difficult, if not at sometimes virtually impossible. Never forget the huge difference of the souls and inner spirit of each. And God tells us in 1 Corinthians 2:14 that we can never discuss Spiritual matters to any degree of understanding or agreement with a *lost man...*

> But the natural man receiveth not the things of the Spirit
> of God: for they are foolishness unto him: neither can
> he know them, because they are spiritually discerned.

If you will keep the diagrams and 1 Corinthians 2:14 constantly in mind, these will help you to stay out of futile disagreements, enhance workplace and other life issues, and to NEVER marry anyone who is an Unbeliever.

OK, let's discuss some pertinent issues more in detail. Once again, one of the most important things I want you to get from the *Born Again man* diagram is that every *child of God* has two (2) souls. Knowing this will remove lots of questions, misunderstandings, and frustration that permeates the lives of far too many Christians. Romans chapters 6, 7, & 8 are three of the most misunderstood and confusing chapters for many Believers. Not if you know and understand the trichotomies. The Holy Scriptures tell us God is not the author of confusion (1 Corinthians 14:33). With the diagram of *Born Again man* showing the battle of the two souls, you can *see* things with your Spiritual eyes and *understand* things with your Spiritual Mind of Christ that most never will. This also gives you clear understanding of just HOW things go on in your life, and

God's Words Bring *Life*

HOW easy it is to move from the temptations and challenges the *old soul* present, BACK to your *new Soul* which is always peace, comfort, and without complications.

The battles between the two souls (2 minds, 2 sets of emotions, 2 wills, 2 *hearts*) get fewer and fewer as you *abandon* to Holy Spirit and His control. In fact, you will *grow in His Grace* (see ch.48) to the point that much of what you used to struggle with has *fallen off* (as my friend Michael Wells put it), and your days will be full of peace, comfort, and joy without any of the consternations, complications, and confusion you might sometimes face today. I think of it as *Christ's LIFE more abundantly* as Jesus spoke of in John 10:10,

> The thief cometh not, but for to steal, and to kill, and to destroy: I am come that they might have life, and that they might have it more abundantly.

That is a beautiful Life of Christ in abundance! (see ch.22). Being Spirit-filled is the imperative to that peaceful, comfortable, and joyous Life.

And never forget that *Christ's LIFE abundantly* can be yours as a Christian that an Unbeliever cannot have. All the *fruit* of Holy Spirit (like His love, joy, peace, faith and all the rest – see ch.35) are unavailable to the *lost*. What a privilege to be one of God's children!

Before we move to the next chapter, let me ask you to think about what the *trichotomy of a Christian in Heaven* looks like. What *falls off* of the *trichotomy of a Believer on earth* and what is *put in place as* we go to Heaven?

And Christ's LIFE abundantly is always fulfilling!

Chapter 9

Mind of Christ

For who hath known the mind of the Lord,
that he may instruct him?
But we have the mind of Christ.
1 Corinthians 2:16

It is beyond many Christians' belief that we possess the actual *Mind of Christ*. But that is primarily because they have never been introduced to and diagnosed the diagram of the *Trichotomy of Born Again man*. Without that knowledge and understanding, they think (with the wrong mind) that they only have one mind (the *natural* mind). And that to possess anything to do with the *Mind of Christ* is to engage in Bible study to fill their *natural* mind with the things of God. I've got news for them. It is actually a Word from God...1 Corinthians 2:14:

But the natural man receiveth not the things of the Spirit

of God: for they are foolishness unto him: neither can

he know them, because they are spiritually discerned.

Well, how about that. The *natural man* only possesses the *natural* mind. With that mind, he receiveth not the things of God, they are foolishness to him, and he cannot know them because they are spiritually discerned. *Lost man* is in a predicament. Yet, *Born Again man* can be in just as bad a predicament, if he is using the *natural* mind still in him instead of the *Mind of Christ*. Wow!

So, listen. If you or I or any Saint chooses to believe using the *natural* mind (which the Holy Scriptures say is *enmity with God* – Romans 8:7), it is no wonder that any Saint could not believe that we actually possess THE *Mind of Christ*. BUT...think and believe with the *Mind of Christ* and love every minute knowing what all that *Mind* brings to our Life!

Therefore (don't you just love that word!), let's list a few great Truths that this *Mind of Christ* gives to us as Saints of God:

revelation – God can reveal in His Mind in us any and all Truth that He sees fit to give us. God's wisdom from Wisdom *(think about that for a moment)* gives us that which our human wisdom is not sufficient for most problems we face.

realization – understanding the great difference between our having the *Mind of Christ* and Sinners not having His Mind. It also includes our being able to grasp and understand fully the things of God.

recognition – being able to see things as God sees them, and knowing when something is not of God.

receiving – being able to receive that which God reveals and gives understanding of…to *own* His revelation to us.

responding – being able to respond to God and His Truth in ways Sinners cannot.

ratiocination – lol, I should leave this one for you to go look up…but it means God has given us His Mind that can use His reasoning and logic to understand and comprehend His Mind, His Emotions, His Will, His Ways, and His Heart.

reaction – God gives us the ability to respond to errors and lies with His Truth.

reconciliation – actually a ministry of Saints to be ambassadors for Christ to share the Gospel and all Truth revealed to us.

relaxation – a mindset capability of Saints (in the Mind of Christ) to rest and relax while facing the most difficult situations or opposition, while the *natural* mind would panic or stress out.

And these are just a few of the wonderful aspects of having this *Infinite Mind* in us where God can reveal to us what He wants us to have at any given moment in time. An intimate walk with God will yield more revelation than we might have ever dreamed possible. And God's revelation supersedes any other discoveries multifold.

T. W. Hunt, a special minister of God who is now in Heaven face-to-face with Christ, once said, "Note the absence in Jesus' Mind of negative emotions such as pessimism, discouragement, doubt, cynicism, suspicion, and gloom. He had no phobias. Jesus never worried about the problems of His life." Wow! There are so many things (like those just mentioned) that come from the *wrong* mind, *wrong* emotions, the *natural* mind, *natural* emotions! And too many Christians accept these as *normal* thoughts and feelings they have to deal with.

Let me give you 17 virtues that are Truth of the *Mind of Christ* that Hunt points out in his study of the *Mind of Christ*:

> But the wisdom that is from above is first *pure,* then *peaceable, gentle,* and *easy to be entreated,* full of *mercy* and *good fruits,* without *partiality,* and without *hypocrisy.* James 3:17
> But the fruit of the Spirit is *love, joy, peace, long-suffering, gentleness, goodness, faith, meekness, temperance:* against such there is no law. Galatians 5:22-23

Beautiful! But, listen to what Hunt had to say about these… "Each of these lists is complete in itself. Each demonstrates perfect unity within itself. But, can the two lists harmonize with one another? The virtues in James are all *adjectives*, and those in Galatians are all *nouns*. I decided to apply each of the *adjectives* (James) to each of the *nouns* (Galatians) to determine if the combinations made sense. Does it make sense to talk about a *pure love, peaceful love, gentle love,* or *entreatable love?* It certainly does! You may also talk about a *lovely peace, loving joy, peaceful gentleness, longsuffering mercy, faithful honesty,* and many other combinations…I saw that the *Mind of Christ* is an integrated mind – it has order, harmony, and unity. Each virtue works perfectly with all other virtues. In fact, the virtues enhance one another. The *Mind of Christ* has no inner conflicts."

Wow! NO INNER CONFLICTS. Can you see that IF a Christian EVER has any *inner conflict* there is a need to immediately stop, move from the *natural* mind which is having its way, and *rest* in the *Mind of Christ* where there are NO INNER CONFLICTS! This one realization would do so much to bring the *Peace of Christ* to a conflicted Believer.

T. W. Hunt was someone who walked with God in a way that God revealed so many things to him. We can miss out on much from the *Mind of Christ* if not walking with God like T. W. did. But, I want what T. W. showed is ours, don't you?!?

By the way, let me give you one more reason we can *know* (intuitively, and many times experientially), that we have the *Mind of Christ*. God tells us in Colossians that as Saints we are *complete* in Christ (that will be covered completely in chapter 26). But for now, let me ask you, IF we are *complete* in Christ…have all of Him…got all of Him at salvation…got Holy Spirit completely, HOW did we NOT get His Mind? Gotcha. Fundamentals. Foundations. They always take us to Truth.

Isn't it interesting that we find it too easy to slip FROM the *Mind of Christ* over to the *natural* mind? Let us always stay alert until we *train ourselves* to *stay* in the *Mind of Christ*. Or, at least quickly recognize when we have moved over! I ask God to keep me in *His Mind*.

And the Mind of Christ is ours. Let us Live in It!

Chapter 10

Wise Beyond Your Years

A wise man will hear, and will increase learning;
and a man of understanding shall attain unto wise counsels.
Proverbs 1:5

Barbara found a study of wisdom in Proverbs and led her Ladies Sunday School class to do the study. It is a life-changer. The authors, Kenneth Boa and Gail Burnett. The study, *Pursuing Wisdom.* I hope you will make every effort to get the workbook and do this study yourself.

Three things stand out the most to me about this study: first, the recognition of the different kinds of *fools* mentioned throughout the Book of Proverbs. Four different Hebrew words are used:

pathim – naïve or simple
kesilim – dull or lacking sense
evilim – actively opposing wisdom
litsim – scoffers or scorners

Let me tell you that ever since doing this study with a Men's SS Class, I have never used the word *simple* anywhere as often or as usual as I once typically did. Wow! Words have meanings. Say what you mean, and mean what you say.

Second, their definition of *wisdom: the outworking of the knowledge of truth.* To soak on this definition and its application led to discovering Boa and Burnett showing how *wisdom* is an *action*, not knowing something...even knowing a whole lot of something. The *wise* WILL hear, increase learning, and seek wise counsels, but the *wise* ultimately put what they have learned to use. The Hebrew for *wisdom* is *chokmah*, and relates to *developing a skill.* There is much to be learned about *skillful* and *wisdom* in this study by Boa and Burnett.

Third, Boa and Burnett go to great length to show and explain the various words like *wisdom, wise, instruction, understanding, knowledge, judgment, discretion, learning, and counsel* – all appearing in the first seven verses of Proverbs chapter 1, and all which are sometimes co-mingled, used in a manner by unlearned teachers or anyone in a typical conversation where we might be led to think they all mean virtually the same thing. Ever since leading that study in the Men's class, I have tried to be diligent to know the difference and use each as truthfully appropriate.

Well, let me give you the first seven verses of *Proverbs 1* before I point out the primary reason for this chapter:

> The proverbs of Solomon the son of David, king of Israel: To know wisdom and instruction; to perceive the words of understanding; To receive the instruction of wisdom, justice, and judgment, and equity; To give subtlety to the simple, to the young man knowledge and discretion. A wise man will hear, and will increase learning; and a man of understanding shall attain unto wise counsels: To understand a proverb, and the interpretation; the words of the wise, and their dark sayings. The fear of the LORD is the beginning of knowledge: but fools despise wisdom and instruction. Proverbs 1:1-7

Many would say that last verse is key. I won't disagree. In fact, knowing what *the fear of the LORD* is helps us to *want* God's wisdom (see ch.49). The Hebrew *yirah* is the most often used Hebrew word in Proverbs, and is the one here in verse 7. Boa and Burnett give an enlightening application of our English translation, "the fear of the LORD is the heart-stopping realization of the glory, majesty, and power of God and of His right to absolute sovereignty over His creation. Without this realization, none of us will ever fall on our face before the Almighty."

OK. My primary reason for this chapter, this *Life Verse,* is to bring forth the tremendous need for us to get God's Wisdom. Taking the definition, *the outworking of the knowledge of truth,* we can *know* the Bible from cover to cover, and if we do not *appropriate* any of it in our lives, we have become *fools*. In fact, James says,

> Who is a wise man and endued with knowledge among you? let him show out of a good conversation his works with meekness of wisdom. James 3:13

Here's a good English word to learn the biblical meaning of: *conversation*. Here it is *anastrophe,* meaning behavior. It is not talking about *talking*, but *living, action, works* as James puts it into perspective. It is a manner and style of Life.

So, my desire is for you to become WISE. **Wise beyond your years**. How do you do that? By being careful to examine whether your life is the Life of Christ personified through your earthsuit. His Wisdom showing in your *conversation (behavior/actions)*. One of the best ways is to BE A STUDENT OF PROVERBS, especially the Hebrew behind key English words! AND THEN ask God to Live His Truths through you. Barbara and I have often read one Proverb a day over the years. Try that. There are 31 chapters in the Book of Proverbs. You can read the one corresponding to the day of the month. If you miss one day, or you haven't read them in a few days, just turn to the day which is the same as the day of the month and pick up from there. And it is a good practice to have a notebook where you can make notes as you read. Well, amen.

And gaining God's Wisdom will lift you to be wise (enjoy the outworking of your knowledge of God's Truth) beyond your years!

Chapter 11

The Battle Is For *Which* Mind

Keep your heart with all diligence; for out of it are the issues of life.
Proverbs 4:23

    This is a very profound saying. Meditate on this very diligently. I have briefly mentioned this before now. It is time to explore it in detail. Use the trichotomy diagrams.
    Two things have to be known, understood, and used before this verse can be utilized by a New Testament Believer. First, this is an Old Testament Truth, where all mankind lived out of the *natural soul*. Christ's disciples prior to the giving of Holy Spirit and His Soul at the *New Birth* (actually, first at Pentecost in Acts chapter 2) all lived with the *old man's natural soul*. Second, only when Born Again Believers possessed the two souls did they have the possibility to really choose *which heart*, thereby *which mind*, to Live by. This is my 3rd use of an Old Testament verse for a chapter text. From now on we will be counting on thinking with the *new mind* if an Old Testament verse is used.
    The Hebrew word for *heart* in this verse is *leb*. It is used widely for the feelings, the will, and even the intellect. The description is clearly declaring the *heart* to be the *working* of the *soul*, which consists of the mind, emotions, and will. The problem for Christians is that most have never been taught that all Christians have two souls…two minds, two sets of emotions, and two wills, two hearts. For these unknowing Saints this creates all kinds of dilemmas!
    The word for *Heart* in the New Testament is *kardia*. (capital H for the Heart of Christ). The meaning and use of *kardia* in the NT is the same as the Hebrew word *leb* in the OT. There is an incredible list of attributes in the many NT scriptures where *heart/Heart* is mentioned: thought, reasoning, understanding, love, hatred, joy, fear, will, judgment, affections, anger, and sorrow…to name a few. WHEN we know what

the Holy Scriptures are referring to when they speak of the *heart*, then, and only then, can we fully appreciate Holy Spirit's instructions for our Life, IF we keep in mind *which heart*.

Now, for Unbelievers (a word for those who have never been Born Again) who have only one mind, there is no dilemma. They only think with the *natural mind* they were physically born with, feel with the one set of *emotions* they were born with, and determine with the one *will* they were born with. But, for us Christians who have two souls, it becomes an issue of **which** *heart* are we going to live in. How does the *natural* mind see something, or how does *God's* Mind see it? Now, listen, a Christian not aware of having two souls, will tend to live out of the *natural* mind, emotions, and will they were born with. As a Christian when we become aware that we have a choice whether to live with Christ's Soul, or not, if we choose Christ's Soul, then the issues of Life become Spirit-led and controlled.

Listen up! With the *old, natural mind* trying to lead you astray of God's thinking, God's ways, God's will…stay alert in the *Lord's Mind* to guard against the lust of the flesh, the lust of the eyes, and the pride of life in the world beguiling you with their enticements. Do not allow humanistic standards or materialistic concepts rob you of the finest Truths that will otherwise enrich you.

When the *Heart of God* within us is the storehouse of treasures (see story of Mary in Luke, ch.2 – read carefully, esp. v.19), the impact upon our life is from HIS Mind, Emotions, and Will. Our thinking, feelings, and decisions are incredible! To be *filled with Holy Spirit* (Ephesians 5:18) is when we are Living in Christ's Soul. All the things of God become precious to us. When Christ's Soul is *in charge*, Christ has become the *doer of the Word* (James 1:22). That is how God is honored in our earthsuit.

But, we must keep in mind, God has told us that the issues of life come out of *which heart* we choose to use. Be diligent to choose Christ's Soul, and the issues of your life will be uncomplicated, peaceful, and comfortable…no matter even if you are in a *storm*. Try that out!

Living in the Heart of God is the only way for a Christian to connect with God.

Chapter 12

It Is A Privilege To Be Able To Understand

*Because it is given unto you to know the mysteries
of the kingdom of heaven, but unto them it is not given.*
Matthew 13:11

The Greek for *know* here is *ginosko,* to *know experientially*. God has given Believers the capability to *know experientially* His mysteries, the mysteries of the kingdom of Heaven. Wow! What a blessing! What a privilege! This is to *know experientially* in our Life, and not just to *know intuitively* in our Christ Mind.

Now let me mention one thing that you need to stay aware of: revelation and understanding involve a process. Growing in the Grace of God is a process (see ch.48). Reading the Holy Scriptures, reading these writings of God's Truth, and beginning to *know experientially* what God is giving you *is a process.* Give Him time to reveal and develop Truth in you!

Remember, I never will forget the first time I read these verses in Matthew 13. I was floored! Jesus telling His disciples that He is speaking to the masses in a way that they will not understand. The spiritual implications of this are staggering, far past this one parable of Jesus recorded in Matthew 13.

But for the moment, think that for us as Christians, we are given the privilege of being able to *understand.* We need to comprehend HOW this is. And the answer is simple...go back to the trichotomy diagram of a Believer and think about what is one of the things that having the *Mind of Christ* as Saints could do for us. His Mind in us gives us the capability to *hear* God, *hear what He is saying, understand what He is saying,* and enjoy any other aspect of communication with God.

Now listen! This *hearing* God and *understanding* what He is saying inevitably leads to our sensing and realizing He is our Life. And His Life being our Life IS one of the greatest Supernatural Spiritual mysteries of all time.

What a relationship! What a fellowship! What a privilege! What an opportunity! Holy Spirit, the Author of the Holy Scriptures according to God, lives inside each of us Saints. This is one aspect of what Scripture talks about as His small, still voice. He speaks, and we can hear with the Spiritual ears God has given us, when Sinners around us cannot. And not only can we hear, but we can *understand.*

Understanding is where the mystery unfolds. There are two spirits in this world. That of God, and that of the devil. God tells us that. God tells us to discern between the two. How do we do that? With the *Mind of Christ.* We can know (intuitively or experientially) mysteries that Sinners cannot. We can understand the Spiritual things going on around us when Sinners cannot. This means we have to stay reminded of what we are understanding, but those around us may not be.

Let me take this in a different direction. When reading the Holy Scriptures, we can *see* and *understand* what we are reading when Sinners cannot. God has told us that explicitly in 1 Corinthians 2:14...

> But the natural man receiveth not the things of the Spirit of God: for they are foolishness unto him: neither can he know them, because they are spiritually discerned.

See? With the Spiritual eyes God has given us. The things of the Spirit of God (here we are talking about the Holy Scriptures) cannot be known by those who are Sinners, still *lost* and only having the *natural* mind. They cannot even *receive* His things. Why? Because things of the Spirit of God are Spiritually discerned. Wow!

Do you begin to think about how that should impact how we interact with those if they are not Saints? Spiritual communication, virtually impossible. Wow! We *see, know, & understand Spiritual things* that the *lost* cannot. Think of the ridiculousness of talking about abortion from a Spiritual standpoint with a *lost* person. Think about all of the other Spiritual issues of today. As a Saint, we have a privilege of communicating with God and with each other that is not available to the *lost*.

As you can imagine, I could go on and on with illustrations and applications. Let me encourage you to do that. And do that especially as you live each day with Saints and Sinners. But remember one thing, you can also have the difficulty of communicating with a Saint who is living out of the *natural* mind instead of the *Mind of Christ* (remember, Saints have two minds!). AND…if you or I are not Living out of the *Mind of Christ* within us, but out of the *natural* mind within us, how does that complicate matters?!?

OK, let me get to the issue I mentioned at the start, the Spiritual implications far past this one parable in Matthew chapter 13. What about the rest of the New Testament? Let me revisit that new word, *parabolic*. A *parable* is recognized in literary circles as being an allegory (symbolic representations of real things or persons). A *parable* itself is a short allegorical story used to illustrate a Truth or principle. *Parabolic* is some Truth or principle expressed by a *parable*. If Jesus spoke (Holy Spirit speaking through Him) in *parables* while He was on earth…look at this verse later in Matthew chapter 13:

> All these things spake Jesus unto the multitude in parables; and without a parable spake He not unto them: That it might be fulfilled which was spoken by the prophet, saying, I will open my mouth in parables; I will utter things which have been kept secret from the foundation of the world. Matthew 13:34-35

…then how many other words from Holy Spirit in the rest of the New Testament are *parabolic*? I have an idea but it would blow most people's *natural* mind. It gives a whole new perspective to that old saying, "The Bible is God's love letter to His Saints. And anyone other than a Saint cannot understand what God is saying." Other than *surface* words and *surface* issues, how much of two other people's love letters do we really grasp, if they say some *private* things? How much of the Holy Scriptures are *private* in that sense? One thing we know for sure: the Spiritual things of God are *private*, because He has told us the *natural* man cannot *see*, cannot *understand*, cannot *receive*, cannot *know* the Spiritual things of God. Private, for His Saints. WOW!

Therefore, do not forget what I have told you in this chapter. And do not take it lightly what a PRIVILEGE it is to have the capacity (*Mind of Christ*) to *see, understand, receive, know,* and *spiritually discern* the Spiritual things of God. Just make sure you are Living in the *Mind of Christ* at all times.

And what a privilege it is to be able to know and understand the Spiritual things of God!

Chapter 13

What Is It To *Believe?*

And they said, Believe on the Lord Jesus Christ,
and thou shalt be saved...
Acts 16:31

    This is one of those chapters that stands alone, yet doesn't. You need to read about *faith* as well as *believe* to be able to understand the Word of God as He intends (chapters 13-18). They are two entirely different *words*, from two entirely different *sources*, each having two entirely different *original language words* that are translated from in both the Old and New Testaments, with two entirely different *meanings and usage*. And yet, most people today (Christians and not) co-mingle the two as if they are one word with the same meaning and usage. Confusion and lack of communication result, with most people not even aware of such. (the work of the enemy ever since that day in the Garden).
    It is almost bizarre how many times the Bible records a story where God told the people what He was going to do, or what was coming to pass in the future...and the people went out and did something on their own, contrary to what God had said, or thinking that God would never do it.
    And why is it God's people often tend to think that we should give God a hand in fulfilling His sovereign plans? Two examples: first, the 12 *spies* coming back from the *observation tour* of the Promised Land and 10 of them convincing the people to be afraid of the *giants* and not go in. 2 *faithful* men, Joshua & Caleb, said "Let us go up at once, and possess it; for we are well able to overcome it" (Numbers 13:30). I like their thoughts, don't you? "We are *well able* to overcome it." What had God already told Moses and the people? "Send thou men, that they may search the land of Canaan, which I *give* unto the children of Israel..." (Numbers 13:2, italics my emphasis). God said He was *giving* the land to

His people. *Giving*. It wasn't a matter of whether they could *take* the land, or at least it wasn't supposed to be! Why did they think they were *well able?* Because they *believed* God!

Another example, Rebekah & Jacob plotting to steal the blessing of Esau, the first born, when God had told Rebekah that the elder would serve the younger (totally contrary to the ways of the Jews, which greatly affected Rebekah's *believing* in an interesting way).

The one thing God has always wanted out of His people is for us to simply *believe Him*. *Believe*, a simple word with so many complications due to humans having distorted, counterfeited, or negating God's original meaning. The Truth, as is the case over and over, is wrapped up in the words from the original languages, including a word search that reveals more than just the meanings in many cases.

There is only one Hebrew word translated *believe, believed,* or *believeth* in the Old Testament: 'âman. It is incredible what this word can entail: to build up or support, to foster as a parent or nurse, to render firm or faithful, to trust or believe, and more. But, basically when translated *believe* it can encompass all of those thoughts into one. *Believe*, or *believing*, is more than some easy mental activity. It has a moral entity that involves commitment. And we will find more about that commitment in the next chapter.

In the New Testament there is one predominant word translated *believe, believed, believeth,* & *believers, believest,* and *believing* – the Greek *pisteuo*. The meaning is the same for today as 'âman in the Hebrew meant in the Old Testament. God takes a firm position on the importance of our *believing Him*. It is commonly said that if God repeats something in the Bible, we ought to take notice. Three (3) times in the New Testament God speaks of Abraham *believing Him,* and God gifted Abraham with righteousness as a Spiritual standing (Romans 4:3, Galatians 3:6, and James 2:23). And these are actually references and quotes from Genesis 15:6 where 'âman, *believed*, appears (Abram, Abraham's name before God changed it, "*believed* in the LORD; and He counted it to him for righteousness"). This is the first time *believe* in any form appears in Scripture. Many scholars agree that Genesis 15:6 is the most important verse in the Old Testament! It is a testimony of the doctrine of *justification*, unifying *believers* for all time.

So now, let us look at a couple of my observations about *believing* from a life of over 70 years in this modern age. One is an interesting phenomenon in our country today: young people not seeking the wisdom of older people, not taking advantage of opportunities to interact with older people, avoiding contact and discussions with older people, and in many cases ridiculing older people simply because they are *old*. God speaks to the contrary. Philippians 4:9. Deuteronomy 4:10. 1 Peter 5:5. Exodus 20:12. Leviticus 19:32. Job 32:4. 1 Kings 12:6. To name a few. Too many younger people do not *believe* older people, OR God, have anything that will help them in this life. How tragic.

Another thought is that I am wondering if the mental state of so many in America today is tied to the lack of *believing God*, even ridiculing the things of God. Repeatedly in Romans chapter 1 God speaks of those who "when they knew God, they glorified Him not as God, neither were thankful; but became vain in their imaginations, and their foolish heart was darkened. Professing themselves to be wise, they became fools…wherefore God gave them up to uncleanness…God gave them up to vile affections…God gave them over to a reprobate mind…" (Romans 1:21-22, 24, 26, 28). Well, amen.

So, listen, one good thing to do is to compile a list of the things God has told us, then BELIEVE GOD. God sends tests that are really a test of WHO God is to you, and do you BELIEVE Him? Always continue to TRUST God's Word no matter whether He has brought to pass as yet what He told us beforehand. HE WILL.

Let me close with two instances where Jesus spoke about *believing*:

> Then said they unto him, What shall we do, that we might work the works of God? Jesus answered and said unto them, This is the work of God, that ye *believe* on Him whom He hath sent. John 6:29

> Then saith He unto Thomas, Reach hither thy finger, and behold my hands; and reach hither thy hand, and thrust it into my side: and be not faithless *(an unbeliever – the real meaning…my observation)*, but *believing*. And Thomas answered and said unto Him, My Lord and my God. Jesus saith unto him, Thomas, because thou hast

seen Me, thou hast *believed:* blessed are they that have not seen, and yet have *believed.* John 20:27-29

I have come to this point where I think that we need to use the word *trust* more than the word *believe.* With the enemy having worked to *change,* or *counterfeit* the real original meaning of *believe,* we can better communicate what we intend to say by more often saying *trust.*

And to believe (trust) is to be blessed!

Chapter 14

Believe and Receive

But as many as received him, to them gave he power to become
the sons of God, even to them that believe on his name.
John 1:12

We looked at what *believe* or *believing* is in the previous chapter. Now we move onto something that follows when we *really believe/trust*.

RECEIVING BEGINS WITH REALLY BELIEVING. This may not sound too profound, but couple it with a very profound statement from Oswald Chambers (the great preacher-professor-missionary from over 100 years ago and author of the renowned *My Utmost For His Highest,* perhaps the most popular devotional book in all Christianity), "When a man fails in personal Christian experience, it is nearly always because he has not *received* anything." Now we can go back and look more closely at John's statement in verse 12 and notice "believing on His name (the Lord Jesus Christ)" precedes one's *receiving Christ* as Savior. That is an important designation.

Many Christians read the Holy Scriptures, hear sermons and SS lessons, talk to other Christians about God and God's Word…but never *receive* what God has intended them to have. This is simply because they have not *believed God,* or actually have yet to *trust* God. Throughout the years preachers have pounded pulpits and proclaimed: "Believe God! Believe God! Believe God!" And many churchgoers have yet to *believe God,* or actually have yet to *trust* God.

Don't be one of these unbelieving Believers. As our Pastor, John Morgan, said back in 1980 soon after Barbara and I were Born Again: "We Baptists like to say, 'God said it – I believe it – that settles it'. NO! God said it, THAT settles it…we need to believe it!" Do you hear that? God has said it, THAT settles it, and you and I need to *believe* Him. According to Scripture, we don't *receive* until we *believe.*

Great things begin to happen Spiritually when we *really believe God*. That happened to all of us when we *believed* the record God had given of His Son Jesus and His being the propitiation for sin. We *received* salvation after we first *believed God* about Jesus' death paying for our sins, and *trusted* in Christ's atonement for our sins.

As far as *receiving* is concerned, there are four things we do well to consider: 1. we must fully grasp what it means to **receive** from God, 2. we must fully want to **receive** something from God, 3. We must understand when we think we are **receiving**, but we aren't, and 4. We must **receive** what God is offering us.

The Greek word for **received** in John 1:12 is *lambano*. It means *to get hold of*. While the Greek for **received** in John 1:11 is *paralambano*, which means *to receive near…i.e.* simply to *associate with*.

> He came unto His own, and His own received Him not.
> John 1:11

Big difference between the two. In fact, His own didn't even *associate* with Him!

When we *lambano* from God, we *take and grab hold of* what He offers. It becomes ours. We *own* it. It becomes part of us. When we *lambano* Him, we *take and grab hold of* Him! Amen!

So, now, think again what Oswald said. In essence, failing in a personal Christian experience is because we actually refused to **receive** *(lambano)* from God. A lot of folks *receive (paralambano), associate with,* but don't *take and grab hold of,* God or His Truth.

Salvation begins with *taking and grabbing hold of* Jesus and God's offer of trusting in Jesus and His payment for our sin on the Cross. *Living Life as a Christian* is our *seeing* what God is offering (what He reveals to us) and *grabbing hold of it*. IT really is a Person. And far too many Christians never *see* and *understand* that. *It* = Person (the Person of Christ).

There are two more words we need to think about before leaving this powerful Life Verse: the first word, *power*, is the Greek *exousia*. Interestingly, this word has many meanings and most scholars cannot agree upon one in particular as to the use in John's text. Listen to all these: privilege, force, capacity, competency, freedom, authority, jurisdiction, liberty, power, right, strength. Wow! Take your pick. We can just know that any one of these will do us good when we *receive/lambano* Christ. The second word, *name*, the Greek *onoma*. This word is used to reference a name, title, character, and reputation of a person. It can imply one's authority. How many times do we see the statement, *at the Name of Jesus*, in Scripture? His Name is to be hallowed, honored, and revered. Such it is when we *believe on His Name*.

No wonder God tells us that *as many as receive/lambano* Him (Christ), *to them He* (God) *gives power to become His sons (even to those who never physically saw or met Christ) but believe on His Name.* The Apostle Paul told us in Philippians 2:10-11 that "at the name of Jesus every knee should bow…and that every tongue should confess that Jesus Christ is Lord, to the glory of God the Father."

And to *lambano* is to grab hold of Christ!

To grab hold of Christ brings God's power.

Chapter 15

Do We Know What Faith Really Is?

*Now faith is the substance of things hoped for,
the evidence of things not seen.*
Hebrews 11:1

In this day and time, the word *faith* has become sort of a nebulous term far removed from its origin in the Bible. It is sad that when so many hear the word *faith*, or use it, they do not distinguish it from other words that do not mean the same thing. So, I want to point out two things in this chapter. One is the accurate Scriptural meaning and the other is some words it is co-mingled with which distort and destroy its original intended meaning and use. All of these errors and malfunctions lead us to miss one of the greatest and most important Truths God wants us to have: the *substance* & *evidence* of Scriptural Faith.

The English word *faith* comes from the Greek *pistis,* which carries with it a great distinction of *our having been persuaded of something*, not just having a *mental knowledge* of something that we see as good or best. Many Christians stop at this mental aspect and fail to enjoy God at work in their lives. To be *persuaded* of something God has said or something God will do, or something that involves God's capability, is to have been given a gift of *participating* with God in whatever is at hand.

In order to comprehend and understand what Scriptural *Faith* is, we must turn to Galatians 5:22 to see where *faith* comes from (the Source) and how we get it:

> But the fruit of the Spirit is love, joy, peace, longsuffering, gentleness, goodness, *faith…*

Do you see this? Scriptural *Faith*, the *Faith* the Holy Scriptures are always speaking of, the *Faith* God wants us to have, is a *Fruit of Holy Spirit*. This is Fruit that is given to any Saint when Holy Spirit is able to work in one's life. This is a *work* of God, not something we *do*. Faith, as

Fruit of Holy Spirit, is God Himself locking in that which is the *substance* and the *evidence* as in our text of this chapter! It is not just a set of beliefs. It is The Divine Power, not human effort. It results in our having confidence (trust) in anything Divine. We possess Him and can experience Him, but it does not originate with us.

How weak or non-existent are the *beliefs* and *convictions* of today's Christians. How weak or non-existent is the so-called *faith* of today's Christians because of being misled to an error of not knowing what *Scriptural Faith* is.

Let me give an illustration that I heard back in 1980. Adrian Rogers, the great preacher in Memphis whom many said *sounded like what we think God's voice would sound like*, said this: "What one person can talk you into, another person can talk you out of. But anything God talks you into, no person can talk you out of." That is *Divine Power*. That is *Fruit of Holy Spirit*. That is *Almighty God*.

In essence, we must get this, and get it solidly fixed in our life. Scriptural *Faith* is truthfully the *Faith of Christ*. That is what makes it Divine. It is His Faith, not my faith…that is, referring to its Source (see ch.17). It becomes my Faith, your Faith, as it is gifted to us by Holy Spirit. But we must always be cognizant that any *Faith* we have came from Christ, and not from us (nothing we have done, instigated, or originated). We *believe* and *receive*. God gifts us with *His Faith* when we *believe/trust* and *receive*.

Do you want more of the *Faith of Christ?* Believe/trust God. Believe/trust God's Word. Believe/trust and Receive. How important is it that we do this? Read the next chapter.

But, before we go there, let me get to point number two I mentioned at the start…co-mingling. I see it over and over where Saints have let the enemy destroy the accurate Scriptural meaning of *Faith* by co-mingling the word *Faith* with *believe* and *trust,* to the point that these three words mean the same thing to most people. They don't. They are three different words with three different meanings.

Let me illustrate: In law, co-mingling of funds is a breach of trust in which someone mixes funds held in care (usually for another person) with other funds (usually the funds of the person doing the mixing), therefore making it difficult to determine which funds belong to which person (and therefore just how much each person possesses). With the co-mingling of different words originally with different meanings, the co-mingled words lose their truthful meaning and become nebulous (indistinct, vague). Question what I am saying? Check out in your next readings or listenings how often someone will say what we need is *faith*, then in the next breath or sentence speak of how we need to *believe*, or that if our *beliefs* are such we can move on in life. Constant co-mingling has moved us to a point that *believe, trust,* and *faith* all mean the same thing. They do not. God did not intend for us to think such.

And it is Faith, Christ's Faith, that will move mountains…not our believing. Our believing is not our believing when it has become His Faith.

Chapter 16

Faith Is Everything With God

But without faith it is impossible to please Him (God)…
Hebrews 11:6

Faith is everything with God. And why shouldn't it be: it is *His Faith*. This should get our attention every time we see the word *Faith* in the Holy Scriptures, speaking of the *Faith of Christ*.

God tells us we cannot please Him without *Faith,* but knowing that it is *His Faith* He is speaking of gives us a completely different perspective than what most Believers think, believe, or function with. The whole New Testament, but particularly certain bold and demanding verses, tells us we are to Live by His Faith. This book is about *how* to Live with His Faith. Live with a capital L, His Life Living out His Faith in our earthsuits. No wonder *Faith (His Faith) is everything with God.*

We will explore some different aspects of *Faith* in the context of a couple of other verses, but for now let's find out just WHAT *Faith* represents. This in itself is a primary aspect.

The *Faith* God speaks of here is HIMSELF. He gave us this Truth in Galatians 5:22, where He says that *Faith* is one of the Fruit of Holy Spirit. Fruit of Holy Spirit is something of Himself given to Believers when we are abandoned to Him and are trusting in Him to Live His Life through us. To possess Holy Spirit is to possess all of Him, including His *Fruit*. To experience His Fruit is to be abandoned to Him for Him to Live through our earthsuits.

An individual without possessing the Lord Jesus Christ cannot please God. God never wills (desires) for any human being today to not have Him indwelling. But, some choose to reject God's offer of salvation that includes possessing God and having Him indwelling.

In the context and discussion of this verse in chapter 11 of Hebrews everything is relative to Scriptural *Faith* and God being One and the same. Unbelievers can never really be pleasing to God. God has revealed Himself to everyone, but some choose to not believe Him, His Word, His record He has given of Christ.

Now listen, it is imperative to know that the Fruit of Holy Spirit is only realized when we *really believe/trust* God on something. There is a difference in something being IN us, and something being REALIZED by us. Just like a *word from God* comes from revelation, even though that *Word* is in us from our salvation. So through the Exchanged Life (God removed the unbelieving, natural nature/life that was ours from our physical birth and replaced it with His Nature/Life at our New Birth), and our Abiding Life (we are His branches attached to Him, The Vine), we deny that residue of the old life/self and abandon all to Him and His Grace Life Lives through our earthsuit. It might take some soaking on all that to really get it. It will help you to get a better understanding and comprehension of this if you soak on the *Diagrams of Our Trichotomy* until they become Scriptural *Faith* to you.

Keep in mind, the purpose of this book is to share some of the greatest Truths that God has revealed to me. I would be remiss, thoughtless, negligent, and neglectful if I didn't write all these down for you to have for the rest of your Life. These little *goodies* are some of God's most profound and uncomplicated Truths that bring His Life to our Life.

I pray that each Truth can manifest Him to you, in you, and through you.

And Faith, His Faith, is always pleasing to God.

Chapter 17

It's Not My Faith; It's Christ's Faith I Live By!

...the life that I now live in the flesh I live by the faith of the Son of God...
Galatians 2:20

Holy Spirit through the pen of the Apostle Paul has clearly told us that Scriptural *Faith* is the *Faith of Christ*. And, the Life Lived out of our earthsuit is to be *by the Faith of Christ*. Every moment of every day we are to *trust His Faith* to govern all we think (His Mind), say (His Voice), feel (His Emotions), and do (His Will)…in essence, Live out of His Heart.

Do you remember I mentioned in Chapter 1 that the enemy is always trying to steal away Truth from the Saints of God? This verse is one of the most significant illustrations of how that is done. In the King James Version of the Holy Scriptures Holy Spirit is said to have penned through the Apostle Paul these exact specific words: *the life that I now live in the flesh* (Greek: *sarx*. human body; earthsuit) **I live by the faith of the Son of God.** Whose Faith has Paul said he, as a Saint and an Apostle, is living by? Christ's. Not his own (Paul). This is a huge Truth!

Coupled with Galatians 5:22, *Faith* being a *Fruit of the Spirit*, it is unquestionable that God has told us that Scriptural Faith IS His Faith. He is the Source. This must become a constant foundation of our Life! What a gift to have our *believing/trusting God* to be solidified with *His Faith*. THAT is when we are standing on the Solid Rock!

Virtually ALL other translations (counterfeits) say: "The life I now live in the body, I live by faith in the Son of God…" Do you see the terrible lie and distortion of Truth from the King James? The bad translations say we live by faith IN the Son of God. They say we are the source of our faith. It is a nebulous "trusting Christ" for what? They constantly deny the Deity of Christ throughout, and they make Life as a Christian a works religion instead of a relationship and fellowship stemming from a New Birth/New Creation. These bad translations come from false texts (there are more Greek texts than one of the New Testament...that's a trick, isn't it?!?). The false texts all originate from somewhere and someone other than the Holy Spirit *inspired* writers! Think about that. Where did the *inspired* writers live and write from? What Greek language (dialect) did the *inspired* writers use? Takes some diligent research to come to your own conclusion.

So, decide for yourselves. Do you want to drum up enough faith in the Son of God to live by, or do you want to *Live by the Faith of the Son of God, who loved you, and gave Himself for you?* Your choice. And we must not miss the Truth that with the Exchanged, Abiding, Grace Life it is Him Living His Life through our earthsuit, and we are no longer doing the Living (unless...if we move over to the *flesh,* same Greek word, *sarx,* here meaning anything that is opposition to Christ... and let the *residue* of the old life live).

Interestingly, this Truth is an uncomplicated fact that only takes having the Truth in the first place (and that comes from having a King James translation), and then believing and trusting and receiving Christ to provide His Faith for Him to Live through our earthsuit.

I will repeat this God-given principle throughout the book: God speaks, we hear, we believe, we trust, we receive, God gives/provides, God Lives/enacts...through our earthsuit. Once this principle becomes a part of your Life, His Life has become *your* Life.

And the Faith of the Son of God IS Life!

Chapter 18

Christ's Faith Comes By Our Hearing

So then faith cometh by hearing, and hearing by the word of God.
Romans 10:17

We've established that Scriptural Faith is Christ's Faith. And we've established that our Faith is His Faith that He has given us when we *pisteuo,* believe in a manner that involves commitment and trust (that's *really believing*). Now we can establish the Source of Christ's Faith becoming our Faith. The Apostle Paul tells us how in one verse, Romans 10:17. Let's digest this verse to get the full explanation.

So then are words that take us back a verse or more, if we are to get the full context and meaning of what the current verse is telling us.

> The word is nigh thee, even in thy mouth, and in thy heart: that is, the word of faith, which we preach; That if thou shalt confess with thy mouth the Lord Jesus, and shalt believe in thine heart that God hath raised Him from the dead, thou shalt be saved. For with the heart man believeth unto righteousness; and with the mouth confession is made unto salvation. For the scripture saith, Whosoever believeth on Him shall not be ashamed. For there is no difference between the Jew and the Greek: for the same Lord over all is rich unto all that call upon Him. For whosoever shall call upon the name of the Lord shall be saved. How then shall they call on Him in whom they have not believed? and how shall they believe in Him of whom they have not heard? and how shall they hear without a preacher? And how shall they preach, except they be sent? as it is written, How beautiful are the feet of them that preach the gospel of peace, and bring glad tidings of good things! But they

> have not all obeyed the gospel. For Isaiah saith, Lord, who hath believed our report? *So then faith cometh by hearing, and hearing by the word of God.* Romans 10:8-17

Paul gives the context and the process by which Christ's Faith becomes our Faith. Hearing, believing, and receiving. Yet Paul gives us a different look of where *pisteuo* arises: "believe in thine heart." Looking at the trichotomy diagrams we see that when the Holy Scriptures speak of the *heart*, they are speaking of the interaction of the components of the *soul* (the mind, emotions, and will). This verifies that to *believe (pisteuo)* involves more than just the mind, a mental assent.

The Greek for the English *hearing* is *akoe*. Its basic meaning is simply to hear with the ear. In the context of *hearing the gospel* it involves the root word, *akouo*, which involves understanding, or hearing with the ear of the mind. Something Supernatural occurs in the hearer when the Gospel Light shines through to the mind that beforehand has been blinded by the god of this world.

> But if our gospel be hid, it is hid to them that are lost: In whom the god of this world hath blinded the minds of them which believe not, lest the light of the glorious gospel of Christ, who is the image of God, should shine unto them. 2 Corinthians 4:3-4

It is the miracle of the power of God (the Gospel) to open the *ear to hear* that allows the *believing in thine heart* to come about, that leads to the *receiving* of the Word of God that results in Christ's Faith becoming real to us.

Granted, there is more here in these verses than just the issue of *hearing, believing, trusting, receiving,* and *Faith*. I hope you will take the time to soak on the totality of what Paul mentions...we must be proclaimers of Christ and God's Truth, speak up and speak out. People will *hear, believe,* and *receive* something from God that becomes their *Faith*. Paul also emphasizes that all Scriptural Faith comes from the Word of God. His Word is the foundation to all we need to believe, trust, receive, and then be rewarded with His Faith to seal our initial believing. The just shall Live by His Faith – sealed belief and trust we can rest on and be assured of, and Live.

Now, listen! Anytime we BELIEVE (*pisteuo*) GOD, He imparts HIS FAITH to us. His Faith confirms and *puts in concrete* that which we have believed, trusted and received from Him. But, don't forget, God has to *say* it before it is something that we can *believe, trust,* and then *receive* His Faith. Scriptural Faith is not just our believing something or anything and claiming we have *faith*.

And the hearing ear is a gift from God!

Chapter 19

Trust Is the Turning Point

Trust in the LORD with all thine heart;
and lean not to thine own understanding.
In all thy ways acknowledge Him, and He shall direct thy paths.
Proverbs 3:5-6

This is, by far, one of my most favorite *Life Verses*. It really gives an uncomplicated plan for *Life as a Christian*. However, we must know beyond a shadow of a doubt just what God is talking about when He says *trust in the LORD with all thine heart*. This is not with any *maybe* or *if* attached.

The Hebrew word translated *trust* in the English is *batach*. And it is not some easy believe-ism or 1st-grade mental assent. In the context here it involves an *attachment of oneself to another*. It involves us attaching ourselves to God in an unlimited way and manner. We must abandon our all to God where we are completely dependent on Him. *Dependency* is synonymous with *trust*. Some other ways of describing this dependency involve our feeling safe with God, our being confident with God, our total reliance on God. This IS the *turning point* in our Life as a Christian. No matter how carelessly someone defines or has some sort of idea of what *believe* is, TRUST takes the fellowship to an entirely higher level.

Some folks say they *believe* airplanes are safe to travel in, BUT they do not *trust* one enough to climb aboard. See the difference. See how important it is for us to *trust in the LORD with all our Heart*? And, keep in mind what the totality of the *Heart* represents.

Our dependency can be on something He has said, or on something He is capable of doing, or on something He has promised, and any other necessary way for us to be dependent upon Him. God is simply telling us to be dependent upon Him with all our Christ-Heart.

But here is the absolute kicker for me: He is the One who is Omniscient. He is the One with a 999 trillion+ IQ, and we are limited to 150 or less. Therefore, why would we *lean on our own understanding* instead of leaning on His Omniscience?

Listen to what God gives as a follow-up in Proverbs 3:
> Be not wise in thine own eyes: fear the LORD, and depart from evil. It shall be health to thy navel, and marrow to thy bones. 3:7-8

Those are beautiful words, aren't they! First of all, when we in any way are *wise in our own eyes* it involves thinking with our pitifully weak and limited *natural* mind. Oh, how pride can take us to a pinnacle of belief and trust that WE are so smart. Oh, yeah, 100+ vs 999 trillion+? (I used to use *kazillion* in an illustration, but folks' eyes start spinning trying to wrap their 100+ mind around what a *kazillion* is…lol.). Do you see how foolish it is for us to even consider *our own understanding* about anything instead of leaning on God's? Let me remind you of that excellent study of *Pursuing Wisdom* by Larry Boa and Gail Burnett about the *fools* in Proverbs. It will make you see why King Solomon wrote so much about our avoiding being a *fool*.

Let me close with this truth: Barbara and I learned long ago that the smartest thing we could do in making any decision was to *trust in the LORD with all our heart, and lean not to our own understanding…and in all our ways acknowledge Him and wait for Him to direct our paths.*

Did you notice a new word there? *Wait.* That is another aspect of the end result that we will look at some other time. We pray you will learn to always *trust in the LORD with all thine heart!*

And trust is a serious commitment of the Christ-Heart within us!

Chapter 20

The Man of the Holy Scriptures Brings Life, Not the Words

> Search the scriptures; for in them ye think ye have eternal life:
> and they are they which testify of Me.
> And ye will not come to Me, that ye might have Life.
> John 5:39-40

It is very important for me to expound on something I mentioned a couple of times in the first chapter: *all Scripture is to take us TO Christ*. This means we are not to stop at the words, but get to The Word.

> In the beginning was the Word, and the Word was with God, and the Word was God. John 1:1
>
> In Him was Life; and the Life was the Light of men. John1:4
>
> That which was from the beginning, which we have heard, which we have seen with our eyes, which we have looked upon, and our hands have handled, of the Word of Life; 1 John 1:1

With the Word, we have God. God in an earthsuit was Jesus Christ. God in Spirit is Holy Spirit. And one of the foundational Beings of the Trinity is LIFE. They declare this. They are Eternal Life. We have Life, Eternal Life, because of our New Birth. Let us think for the moment on one thing: God wants us to know and to focus on His Truth that His Life is to be our Life, not His words. His words are Spirit and Life (John 6:63) – see ch. 2 – but, they speak of Him and are able to take us to Him, His Life. The Holy Scriptures are for us to discover and to begin to Live (experience) His Life (actually Him Living it through our earthsuit).

So, we must always keep in mind that the Word of God is not a compilation of some words, verses, chapters, and books that we get to read, and perhaps memorize, and then head out the door to go and *try to live* those words. The Word of God is actually Life, the Word…Jesus. And in this day and time, for Believers, He is Holy Spirit IN US. His LIFE IN US.

Think about this for one moment: Why would we as Saints of God with God (Holy Spirit) Living inside our earthsuit want to expend one ounce of natural thought or energy to be or do whatever, when He wants to BE and DO through our earthsuit?

Which means that what His intentions are relate to His LIFE being Lived out through our earthsuit. And we get to enjoy His LIFE. Our continuous journey should be one of discovering more and more of His LIFE that is ours for the receiving (this can be done by reading the Holy Scriptures to find *Life Verses* that show us His LIFE for us).

Every *Life Verse* will show us something Holy Spirit will *do* through us if we are aware of this LIFE benefit, desire this LIFE benefit, and abandon to His Life being Lived through our earthsuit. The latter is being Spirit-filled. The only way to *Live Life as a Christian* God's Way is to do so Spirit-filled. Any other way is not the Way.

One thing that is a constant Truth throughout this book is this: WE are not to live *the Christian life*. Holy Spirit desires to Live His LIFE through our earthsuit. Several years ago I quit using the phrase *the Christian life* and began to speak of *Life as a Christian*. The focus since then has always been Christ's LIFE being MY LIFE (ch.21 will detail this for you). Yes, there are physical activities (that which are relating to this world contrasted with the Spiritual) that I perform in my earthsuit. But the Life we are talking about God Living through us is the Spiritual. Keep in mind, there are many things we may consider physical but are actually Spiritual: love, kindness, attentiveness…the list is long.

And Jesus always brings His LIFE!

Chapter 21

CHRIST's Life Is MY Life

When Christ, who is our life…
Colossians 3:4

There could not be a more definitive and pointed message to ALL Believers about *Life as a Christian* than our text verse for this chapter. We have bounced all around this crucial statement in the previous chapters, but here I will get straight to the point, hit the nail on the head as my grandpa Brad used to say.

Life as a Christian was planned and designed (predestinated to be so) by God for us as His children to *let go and let God*. As an Unbeliever, life (small *l*) is all about self-effort. And the *flesh*, not the physical flesh, but the spiritual (small *s*) *flesh* – the Christian's *old* ways of the *old soul* which still reside in Believers, that which is opposition to God – is always a failure at life. The only person to Live life on earth as God intended, once Adam & Eve sinned and brought on the *fall*, was Jesus who Lived Life in an earthsuit as God had originally planned for mankind.

When we know this and believe the reality of it, we abandon ourselves to Him, and Holy Spirit takes over and the *Life of Christ* becomes our Life here on earth. THAT is what God means when He told us *Christ, who is our life*. It is not US living it; it is Christ Living in our earthsuit.

There are many things God has told us that we can believe and trust easily. There are other things that seem to take us longer to reach a belief and trust in God about. And there are some things that seem to escape most Christians completely. This Truth we are examining in this chapter is one of the latter.

The one factor too many Believers forget (or, fail) to *do* is simply *believe, trust, and receive from God*.

If God has told us Christ is our Life, what is there for us to *do* other than *believe, trust, and receive His Life?* When we *believe God*, He solidifies our *believing* with His FAITH, *fruit* of Holy Spirit. When He has gifted us with His FAITH, then His LIFE can begin to function through us. This is what we would call *letting go and letting God* Live His LIFE in our earthsuit. Christianity, or *Life as a Christian*, is uncomplicated and practical with a Believing Believer. It gets very complicated and not practical at all with an Unbelieving Believer. We must choose which we will be.

All that His LIFE can be in our earthsuit is what this book is about. Each Truth is a Life Verse that shows us the potential of His LIFE for us. All you have to do is learn the Truths, *believe* them, *trust* them, *receive* them, *abandon self*, and enjoy His LIFE.

Now, have you ever wondered about how we will get to Heaven, and what we will be like in Heaven? Christ's LIFE will be our Life in Heaven. It will be us, but His LIFE, the Supernatural. It is reality that God hasn't given us as much information about Life there as opposed to the great amount of information about Life here. But, we just *believe Him* and look forward to whatever He has planned for us there…just like He planned for us here. Jesus did give us a glimpse of sorts…

> I am the resurrection, and the life: he that believeth in me, though he were dead, yet shall he live: And whosoever liveth and believeth in me shall never die. Believest thou this? John 11:25-26

Isn't that great?!? Believeth in Him (and we know that is more than just a mental belief), and though we die the physical death, we shall live and never die (the Supernatural Spiritual Life of Christ). *His LIFE is our LIFE*. I hope you don't ask me to fully explain that. I just *believeth Him*.

And believing God always makes a way for the Supernatural to come about!

Chapter 22

Christ's LIFE More Abundantly

> ...I am come that they might have life,
> and that they might have it more abundantly.
> John 10:10

Here is a great example of one word that should begin with a capital letter, so as to indicate that it is a part of God. If *life* in this verse were shown as *Life* (Christ's *Life*, as the verse is speaking of), then so many wrong thoughts and ideas and endeavors could be avoided. Christians would not be trying to *get* a life of abundancy of *things*, as most interpret this verse to say with the little *l* in *life*. No, they would be seeking to get all of Christ's *Life* that Jesus said He came that we His brethren might have, and have abundantly. That, is our joint-heirship (Romans 8:17)...for today!

So, how do we begin to enjoy Christ's *Life* more abundantly? Well, the battles between the two souls (2 minds, 2 sets of emotions, 2 wills...2 *hearts*) get fewer and fewer as you abandon to Holy Spirit and His control. In fact, you will *grow in His Grace* (see ch.48) to the point that much of what you used to struggle with has *fallen off* (as my friend, Michael Wells, put it), and your days will be full of peace, comfort, and joy without any of the consternations, complications, and confusion you might sometimes face today. This is *Christ's LIFE more abundantly* as Jesus spoke of in John 10:10,

> The thief cometh not, but for to steal, and to kill, and to destroy: I am come that they might have life, and that they might have it more abundantly.

That is a beautiful *Life of Christ* in abundance! Being Spirit-filled is the imperative to that peaceful, comfortable, and joyous Life, Christ's *Life* of abundance. The thief (devil) has only one work in any Believer: to try and steal, kill, and destroy Christ's Abundant Life that is our heritage.

And never forget that *Christ's LIFE abundantly* is yours as a Christian that an Unbeliever cannot have. All the *fruit* of Holy Spirit (like His Love, Joy, Peace, Faith and all the rest) are unavailable to the *Lost*. What a privilege to be one of God's children!

It really is interesting and amazing how many verses from Scripture become erroneous teachings. How? Because of careless reading, and liberal teaching (and perhaps erroneous translations from false texts). Too many Believers *get a word from God* from teachers and preachers rather than from God (Holy Spirit)!

John 10:10 is a prime example. What is the common misunderstanding, misbelief and incorrect interpretation of what Jesus was saying? That He wants us to have an *abundant life*, to which many then start making a *list* of what an *abundant life* would look like to them. Why that? Because it fits into the masses *whose god is their belly* (Philippians 3:19) and their desire for *more* (more things). Forget what God's Word truthfully says.

Look close at this verse: "I am come that they might have **life**, and have **it** (Christ's *Life*) more abundantly." The context clearly and literally, LIFE more abundantly, NOT a more *abundant life*. BIG DIFFERENCE! Remember, it is the *Life* of Christ that MAKES us a Christian. Multiple verses tell us this. His *Life* in a person differentiates that person from the one who does not possess His *Life*.

> But if the Spirit of Him that raised up Jesus from the dead dwell in you, He that raised up Christ from the dead shall also quicken your mortal bodies by His Spirit that dwelleth in you. Romans 8:11
>
> If ye then be risen with Christ, seek those things which are above, where Christ sitteth on the right hand of God. Set your affection on things above, not on things on the earth. For ye are dead, and your life is hid with Christ in God. When Christ, who is our life, shall appear, then shall ye also appear with Him in glory. Colossians 3:1-4
>
> As ye have therefore received Christ Jesus the Lord, so walk ye in Him. Colossians 2:6
>
> I am crucified with Christ: nevertheless I live; yet not I, but Christ liveth in me: and the life which I now live in

the flesh I live by the faith of the Son of God, who loved
me, and gave Himself for me. Galatians 2:20
Now if any man have not the Spirit of Christ, he is none
of His. Romans 8:9
He that hath the Son hath life; and he that hath not the
Son of God hath not life. 1 John 5:12

There is no denying the Truth of Christ's *Life* being so much more important and critical than any kind of prosperity or abundance of *things* for any Believer. So the whole idea of living *Life as a Christian* hinges on Christ's *Life* as the foundation. In fact, that is why I no longer use the term *the Christian life*. Why? It begs a LIST of *do this, don't do that, get this, get that, have this, have that* on each individual Christian's life. *Life as a Christian* focuses on Christ's *Life* as *our Life* and all God does for each Believer.

It is high-time that all Christians get back to the basic Truth: Christianity is all about Christ, not the Christian. Christianity is all about Christ's Life in Believers, not Believers having an abundance of things, activity, etc…and calling that an *abundant life*. Believers are privileged to participate in the *Life of Christ* while still on this earth, and in the afterlife. *Life* forever with God in Heaven and the New Jerusalem is in reality our *Life* NOW.

Christianity began when God came in an earthsuit through the miraculous conception and resulting physical birth of Jesus Christ. (keep in mind, our Lord Jesus Christ had been around before creation – John 1:1). Christianity really became known when the adult Jesus walked and talked, healed and did many miracles, and ultimately was crucified on His Cross. Believers were first acknowledged as being people of *The Way*. Remember Jesus' declaration?

Jesus saith unto him *(Thomas)*, I am *the way*, the truth, and
the life: no man cometh unto the Father, but by me. John
14:6 *(italics my emphasis and Thomas' name for identification)*

Saul, later who became the Apostle Paul, was breathing out threatenings and slaughter against the disciples of Jesus, and desired of the High Priest:

And Saul, yet breathing out threatenings and slaughter
against the disciples of the Lord, went unto the high
priest, and desired of him letters to Damascus to the

> synagogues, that if he found any of this *way*, whether they were men or women, he might bring them bound unto Jerusalem. Acts 9:1-2 *(italics my emphasis)*

It was first at Antioch that Believers were called *Christians*, years after the crucifixion.

> Then departed Barnabas to Tarsus, for to seek Saul: And when he had found him, he brought him unto Antioch. And it came to pass, that a whole year they assembled themselves with the church, and taught much people. And the disciples were called *Christians* first in Antioch. Acts 11:25-26 *(italics my emphasis)*

Now they were called Christians. From Christ. Believers and followers of Christ. They were the first to learn of *Christ in them*, and to begin to experience His LIFE through them, *abundantly*. How? Boldness in the Gospel being proclaimed to others. Boldness in being persecuted in Christ's Name. Boldness in His *Life* as they saw Him *Living* through themselves in miraculous ways.

The question for us today is are we experiencing His LIFE in any similar ways? (Virtually every chapter from now to the end of this book IS an example of *experiencing Christ's LIFE more abundantly*).

And experiencing Christ's LIFE IS The Way!

Chapter 23

Branches On The Vine

> I am the vine, ye are the branches...
> John 15:5

In five verses (John 15:1-5) God gives us one of His most dramatic pictures of the relationship and fellowship He designed for Himself with His children. In fact, these are some of the most crucial verses telling us of the assurance of our salvation and the guarantee of Eternal Life. Jesus loved speaking and teaching in parables, and this is one of His greatest.

(I like to think of the picture of the Vine & the branches as one of God's two best pictures of Christianity, along with the Shepherd & sheep pictures – Psalm 23 and John 10)

Every botanist (a biologist specializing in the study of plants) should love the picture God paints in the first five verses of John 15...

> I am the true vine, and my Father is the husbandman. Every branch in me that beareth not fruit he taketh away: and every branch that beareth fruit, he purgeth it, that it may bring forth more fruit. Now ye are clean through the word which I have spoken unto you. Abide in me, and I in you. As the branch cannot bear fruit of itself, except it abide in the vine; no more can ye, except ye abide in me. I am the vine, ye are the branches. He that abideth in me, and I in him, the same bringeth forth much fruit; for without me ye can do nothing. John 15:1-5

There are several Truths in these five verses. Let me encourage you to make the time to do extensive study of these verses and especially their context with the plant world. Learning from a real botanist, or a learned gardener, could be a great help to understanding your fellowship with God, your Life's Husbandman.

For now, let me point out a couple of basic things that should mean so much to you. First, make sure you understand that Jesus is speaking of Himself being *our* Vine. We are branches in Him. That may take a moment's meditation to soak on what that really means. But, as a Christian, a *new creation* of God, we are *attached* to Him in a very special way. Secondly, our *attachment* is *permanent*. This speaks of the assurance of our salvation and the guarantee of Eternal Life. It is His LIFE in us that is our Eternal Life. Our Life in Him will continue to Live eternally with Him when this physical life is done. Amen!

There is more! As a *branch of the Vine* we get Life and all that is needed for that Life *from Him*. This can get so exciting it makes me want to shout a "hooooooooo-boy!" at any moment, and on many moments. *Life as a Christian* (my favorite way of expressing what our Life is as this *new creation*) is not dependent on me supplying the Life, but His Life flowing through my earthsuit. And yours. Ask any botanist and they will tell you the vine is the source (Christ is our Source) of all the branch's need for life. The branches are constantly receiving (as attached…which is *abiding*) from the vine.

So, you can see there is so much to this *new creation* and *branches in the Vine* story God is telling us. We will continue to look for more as each chapter unfolds…

And the Vine keeps pouring LIFE out to us!

Chapter 24

In Christ

Blessed be the God and Father of our Lord Jesus Christ,
who hath blessed us with all spiritual blessings
in heavenly places in Christ.
Ephesians 1:3

In one verse the Apostle Paul introduces the magnitude of God's plan and purpose of *His indwelling* His Children, called Saints, Christians or Believers. Just the uncomplicated, practical knowledge and understanding of all Holy Spirit shares through Paul about the fellowship of Christ *in us* and us *in Christ* is the foundation ALL Believers need for *undergirding* this *Life as a Christian*. Without it one goes about trying to *get* or *be* ALL they already *have* and *are*. How frustrating it is to *work* for what one already has and can't get by *works,* or *working for it.*

So, let's take a look at the next 11 verses to start with, and let me encourage you to carry with you a list of the ways God has given us special Spiritual benefits because we are IN CHRIST. I note in parentheses an identification of the Person of the Godhead Paul is speaking of when using only personal pronouns.

> According as He (God) hath chosen us in Him (Christ) before the foundation of the world, that we should be holy and without blame before Him (God) in love: Having predestinated us unto the adoption of children by Jesus Christ to Himself (God), according to the good pleasure of His (God's) will, To the praise of the glory of His (God's) grace, wherein He (God) has made us accepted in the beloved: In whom (Jesus) we have redemption through His (Jesus') blood, the forgiveness of sins, according to the riches of His (God's) grace; Wherein He (God) hath abounded toward us in all

wisdom and prudence; Having made known unto us the mystery of His (God's) will, according His (God's) good pleasure which He (God) hath purposed in Himself (God). That in the dispensation of the fullness of times He (God) might gather together in one all things in Christ, both which are in heaven, and which are on earth; even in Him (Jesus). In whom (Jesus) also we have obtained an inheritance, being predestinated according to the purpose of Him (God) who worketh all things after the counsel of His (God's) own will: That we should be to the praise of His (God's) glory, who first trusted in Christ. In whom (Christ) ye also trusted, after ye heard the word of truth, the gospel of your salvation: in whom (Jesus) also, after that ye believed, ye were sealed with that Holy Spirit of promise, Which is the earnest of our inheritance until the redemption of the purchased possession, unto the praise of His (God's) glory. Ephesians 1:4-14

WOW! I remember starting to build a Life of praise, joy, confidence, witnessing, prayer, counseling, discipleship and enjoyment of *who I was in Christ* after my *New Birth*.

There are other passages and individual verses that give us much more of *our inheritance*. Listen to what Paul told the Ephesians later on:

For through Him (Christ) we both have access by one Spirit unto the Father. 2:18

For this cause I bow my knees unto the Father of our Lord Jesus Christ, of whom (Christ) the whole family in heaven and earth is named, that He (God) would grant you, according to the riches of His (God's) glory, to be strengthened with might by His (God's) Spirit in the inner man; That Christ may dwell in your hearts by faith; that ye, being rooted and grounded in love, May be able to comprehend with all saints what is the breadth, and length, and depth, and height; and to know the love of Christ, which passeth knowledge, that ye might be filled with all the fullness of God. Now unto Him (God) that is able to do exceeding abundantly above all that we ask

or think, according to the power that worketh in us,
Unto Him (God) be glory in the church by Christ Jesus
throughout all ages, world without end. Amen. 3:14-21

Again...WOW! And again, these are just the beginning of all God's revelation about our Life IN Christ. Here is a list of these and more...

I am God's child. 1 Peter 1:23
> for I am Born Again of the incorruptible seed of the Word of God which liveth and abideth forever

I am a member of God's family. Ephesians 3:15, 5:30
I am joined with all Believers (not inferior to any). Galatians 3:8-9
I am a partaker of the promise. Galatians 3:6-7; Ephesians 3:6
I am alive (formerly a dead spirit in sins). Ephesians 2:5
I am raised up with Christ. Ephesians 2:6
I am chosen, holy, and blameless before God. Ephesians 1:4
I am God's workmanship created in Christ Jesus. Ephesians 2:10
I am seated in Heaven already. Ephesians 2:6
I am forgiven of all my sins, past-present-future. Ephesians 1:7; 1 John 2:12
I am washed in the blood of Christ. Hebrews 9:14; 1 Peter 1:18-19
I am a new creation. 2 Corinthians 5:17
I am the temple of Holy Spirit. 1 Corinthians 6:19
I am a Saint. Romans 1:6-7; 1 Corinthians 1:2
I am ransomed (restored to favor). 1 Timothy 2:6
I am justified and redeemed. Romans 3:24
I am the righteousness of God. 2 Corinthians 5:21
I am now Light. Ephesians 5:8
I am free from my old man (crucified). Romans 6:6
I am free from any condemnation. John 5:24; Romans 8:1
I am free from the law of sin and death. Romans 8:2
I am liberated. Galatians 2:4, 3:24-25, 5:1,13
I am sanctified (holy, set apart). 1 Corinthians 1:2
I am set free from sin and the past. John 8:36; Romans 6:2,11
I am always led in Christ's triumph. 2 Corinthians 2:14
I am strong in the Lord. Ephesians 6:10; Philippians 4:13
I am a joint heir with Christ. Romans 8:17
I am a son and an heir. Galatians 4:7

I am sealed with Holy Spirit unto the day of Redemption. Ephesians 1:13
I am complete in Christ. Colossians 2:10
I am alive with Christ. Ephesians 2:5; Colossians 2:12-13
I am accepted in the Beloved. Romans 15:7; Ephesians 1:6
I am born of God, and sin not, and the evil one does not touch me. 1 John 5:18
I am blessed with all spiritual blessings. Ephesians 1:3
I am wisdom, righteousness, sanctification, and redemption. 1 Corinthians 1:30
I possess ALL of Christ via Holy Spirit. Romans 8:9-11
I have a Heart and Mind guarded by the peace of God and Christ Jesus Philippians 4:7
I have all my needs supplied. Philippians 4:19
I have boldness and confident access to God by the faith of Christ. Ephesians 2:18, 3:12
I live by the faith of Christ. Galatians 2:20
My Life is hidden with Christ in God. Colossians 3:3

What more could I *want* ?
> Let me include a personal note: This Truth (who I am IN CHRIST) came to me not very long after we were Born Again. I began to look around, listen to other Christians talk, and I came to realize that very few had ever come to know this Truth, much less Live in enjoyment of it. It has been a mainstay of my Life as a Christian, and to share the manifestations of this Truth in any ministry I have had.

And knowing who we are IN CHRIST leads the way to His Life of victory!

Chapter 25

Christ In Us

> To whom God would make known
> what is the riches of the glory
> of this mystery among the Gentiles;
> which is Christ in you, the hope of glory.
> Colossians 1:27

It is interesting that for the first 15 years or so after being Born Again all I knew, or really thought much about, was *who I was in Christ*. My personal living, my preaching, my teaching, my counseling…all centered around that. And then Barbara and I went to a retreat with some friends, to Colorado Springs, Colorado. It was held at a beautiful place called Glen Eyrie, the home of the Navigators Ministry. The originally-planned speaker had a family emergency arise and could not make it. Enter Michael Wells as the speaker.

I know it wasn't the first time I had read or heard this verse, but it was one of those Divine moments when God reveals something to us that heretofore has not been *seen*. *Christ IN us, the hope of glory*. And all that is intended to mean to each and every Christian, and all that can perhaps mean to everyone we come into contact with. Think about both of those aspects!

Sadly, virtually every Christian I have known has seen this verse to mean simply *Christ in us, our hope **for** glory*, in the next life. That is not ALL the Truth. He is **for** NOW also!

Christ is our everything
when it comes to *Living Life as a Christian*.
…*for without Me ye can do nothing*. John 15:5

He is our Divine Nature. 2 Peter 1:4
He is our Life. Colossians 3:1-4; John 14:6
He is our Grace of all done in our life. 1 Corinthians 15:10
He is our Eternal Life. 1 John 5:13
He is our Captain of our Salvation. Hebrews 2:10
He is our Earnest of our Inheritance. Ephesians 1:14
He is our Sanctification. 1 Corinthians 1:30
He is our Wisdom. 1 Corinthians 1:30
He is our Righteousness. 1 Corinthians 1:30
He is our Redemption. 1 Corinthians 1:30
He is our Good Works. Ephesians 2:10
He is our Way. John 14:6
He is our Truth. John 14:6
He is our Joy. John 15:11; Galatians 5:22
He is our Peace. John 14:27; Galatians 5:22
He is our Love. John 15:9-10; Galatians 5:22; 2 Timothy 1:7
He is our Long-suffering. Galatians 5:22
He is our Gentleness. Galatians 5:22
He is our Goodness. Galatians 5:22
He is our Faith. Galatians 5:22
He is our Meekness. Galatians 5:22
He is our Temperance. Galatians 5:22
He is our Power. 2 Timothy 1:7
He is our Sound Mind. 2 Timothy 1:7
He is our Work. Philippians 2:13; 1 Thessalonians 5:24
He is our Deliverer. Hebrews 2:14-15; Psalm 18:2
He is our Fortress. Psalm 18:2; Psalm 91:2
He is our Rock. Psalm 18:2
He is our Refuge. Psalm 46:1; Psalm 91:2
He is our High Tower. Psalm 18:2
He is our Strength. Psalm 18:2; Psalm 46:1; Philippians 4:13
He is our King. John 12:15

Well, this list goes on and on. Christ is our everything when it comes to *Living Life as a Christian*. Now, here is the essence of all this. He wants to Live His Life through our earthsuit. Just as the Father Lived His Life through Jesus' earthsuit. THAT is how *we* get to experience *Life as a*

Christian. THAT is how *we* can impact others, impact this world. And there is no other way. All other ways are not the way. He only is The Way.

It all goes back to our not trying to live, but to let Him Live. It all goes back to our not trying to get something or be someone that we ALREADY have and are! It is tragic that the Gospel message of Salvation and Life is so misrepresented and misunderstood in so many things by many Christians today.

Now let me give you an idea that I am betting you have never thought of… And almost everyone you know has never thought of… We all know that each of us has *something* of our earthly father and mother in us. We came from them. But, what IF they had *actually been totally placed in us*, father in the sons, mother in the daughters. DO WE THINK they perhaps would have *lived our life* differently IF they could have *been in us* and been *given the freedom* to make every choice for us (with their mind in us), and act out in our earthsuit? Wow! Soak on that for a moment or two! And then acknowledge the reality that THIS is what the Omniscient, Omnipotent Christ wants to do in our earthsuit.

Our Lord Jesus Christ came that we might have Life, His Life, *abundantly*, now and for eternity! Imparted to us with the indwelling of Holy Spirit on the grounds of redemption. Now, listen! The Life of God, once clothed on earth by the Man named Jesus, is now clothed again on earth in our earthsuit. It is Truth that the Lord Jesus Christ will Live His Life through each of us on earth today as He Lived His Life in His own earthsuit 2000 years ago…**IF** we abandon our right to our life and let Him Live His Life.

May you get familiar with, and begin to enjoy, these wonderful gifts from God. As I said in the previous chapter, when we learn who we are in His family and begin to appropriate our heritage, we see and experience His LIFE on a higher plane. Until all this becomes a reality in your earthsuit, let me encourage you to carry this *list* with you for as long as it takes for Him to become your Life.

I find that the following communication with God gives me assurance Holy Spirit is providing all of Christ for me in my earthsuit…

Holy Spirit, make known to me, make experiential to me, all that
Christ is in me. Holy Spirit, I choose to allow You to occupy the

whole of my personality, my earthsuit, my being, with the adequacy of Christ. And I trust You to do so and thank You that You will.

And His Life will be all this for you!

Chapter 26

Complete In Christ

For it pleased the Father that in him (Christ) should all fullness dwell;
Colossians 1:19
For in him dwelleth all the fullness of the Godhead bodily.
And ye are complete in him, which is the head
of all principality and power:
Colossians 2:9-10

The revelation of God in these three verses is staggering. First, God tells us that it pleased Himself that in Christ all the fullness of the Godhead dwelt. Actually, that should not surprise any Christian, since Christ WAS God in an earthsuit. Wherever God is, all of God is. He doesn't be anywhere in *pieces*. But, it is important to see God revealing that in Christ in an earthsuit dwelt *all the fullness of the Godhead* (that is ALL the fullness of God the Father, God the Son, and God the Holy Spirit...the three are the *Godhead, deity*). The Greek *pleroma* is a filling, a totality. This is huge in the realm of Christian theology (the study of God, God's fellowship with all of His creation, and more).

Then to top it off, God tells us (Believers) that we are *complete* IN HIM (Christ). The Greek *pleroo* is a performance, an accomplishment. So, (hold onto your seats!) the total accomplishment and Person of performance of the Godhead resides in you and me as Believers! We lack nothing or nobody for Life. God and His LIFE are available to us for Living through us.

So, why do we go to such effort to *be* a Christian? Or, to *try* to be a *good* Christian? We *are* one with Almighty God IN US, in totality! No wonder so many could face extreme persecution and challenges in Bible days. No wonder so many could be martyred for being a Believer. No wonder the same is experienced around the world today. The wonder is how in the Name of Christ can we who are Christians have any worries, fears, or any unbelief?

Ponder for a moment what it means to have *all the fullness of the Godhead* dwelling in you. What do you think of? How does this change the way you will think of things? How does this make you feel? What does this do to the issues and problems you face? How does this affect the decisions you need to make? Does this change the way you look at others? Does this affect the way you interact with others? CAN LIFE TAKE ON A NEW LOOK FOR YOU?

We are exploring so many of the aspects of *the fullness of Christ* and what this means in reality to each Saint day in and day out.

Oh, there is something else in our text verses. Christ is *the Head of all principality and power*. Who can come against the *Head*? Especially a *Head* with such power? So, not only just the fact that He (Who is all that has been mentioned) dwells in us, but He is over ALL that otherwise exists. Tell me, what is our problem that we think is so overwhelming? One of the things we are exploring in more detail is that God has established Himself to BE *our Life* for the rest of our time here on earth (as well as after this Life). To fully appreciate this it takes spending some time soaking on that!

Let me close for now by taking us back a couple of verses from our text in this chapter...

> As ye have therefore received Christ Jesus the Lord, so walk ye in him: Rooted and built up in him, and stablished in the faith, as ye have been taught, abounding therein with thanksgiving. Beware lest any man spoil you through philosophy and vain deceit, after the tradition of men, after the rudiments of the world, and not after Christ. Colossians 2:6-8

For now, let us realize God gave all Believers for all time a revelation of a procedure and a warning prior to His revelation of the *completeness*. We will look at those in detail later on. One thing I have noticed in my years of study...God gives instruction of His LIFE to be Lived through all of His children in clear and precise terms...and the preaching and teaching of today has been erroneous and misled so many to live this life (notice, no capital *L*'s) on our terms, instead of His. It wouldn't hurt for you to take a moment and meditate on verse 6, and ENJOY the staggering *completeness* that is yours right now!

And Christ's completeness will impact your Life!

Chapter 27

The Fullness of God

> That Christ may dwell in your hearts by faith;
> that ye, being rooted and grounded in love,
> May be able to comprehend with all saints
> what is the breadth, and length, and depth, and height;
> And to know the love of Christ, which passeth knowledge,
> that ye might be filled with all the fullness of God.
> Ephesians 3:17-19

I guess we should expect no less than that mouthful when Holy Spirit starts speaking of Saints being filled with all the fullness of God! Wow!

Look at all the things Holy Spirit enunciates: *that Christ may dwell in our hearts by faith* (much more on that later…), *that we would be rooted and grounded in love, that we would be able to comprehend with all saints what is the breadth, and length, and depth, and height* (of His love), and *we would be able to know the love of Christ which passeth knowledge* (wow! there is really something in that point!), AND…*that we might be filled with all the fullness of God.* Whew!

Now, listen, for the sake of the need to fill more chapters with Truths from more great *Life Verses*, I will make this chapter less lengthy than most by including ALL these great revelations in minimized wording in this one chapter. So, let's take them one at a time, from the top…

That Christ may dwell in our hearts by faith.

It is natural for Holy Spirit to say *dwell in our hearts by faith*. Since this would be after we are Born Again (actual moment, and Holy Spirit has imparted Himself and His Faith to us for our Believing in Christ for salvation), His Faith keeps us dwelling in His Heart (of His Soul also imparted to us) and moves us to begin being *rooted and grounded in* (His) *Love.*

That we would be rooted and grounded in love.

His Faith moves us to begin being *rooted and grounded in (His) Love*. Wow! God is Love. Being *rooted and grounded in His Love* is almost incomprehensible, and would be if we didn't have the Mind of Christ to comprehend it. Just imagine. We, as children of God, can have *His Love* be so *rooted and grounded*, solidly implanted and able to *produce Him and His Love* to come forth from our earthsuit.

That we would be able to comprehend with all saints what is the breadth, and length, and depth, and height (of His Love).

His Love gifts us, and enables us, to be able to comprehend a whole lot, especially of *His Love*. Oh, how much there is to comprehend! He has given us the *dimensions*...well, the *directions of the dimensions*. Oh, Lord Jesus, reveal through Your Mind in us ALL of Your Love!

That we would be able to know the love of Christ which passeth knowledge.

Holy Spirit gives an uncomplicated understanding (however, this is one of my most favorite *parabolic* teachings of Holy Spirit). It may appear to say that the Love of Christ passes knowledge, cannot be understood. But, that is not what Holy Spirit is saying. His statement is a *parabolic* expression that confounds the mindset/capabilities of the *natural* mind, BUT, it is not confounding to the mindset/capability of the *Mind of Christ* which we as Saints possess! Holy Spirit says We CAN KNOW the Love of Christ! Know it full well, if we think in *His Mind* in us and get His revelation of it. God's Word tells us there are very few things any Saint could experience that are better than to know full well just what is the Love of God and how much He Loves us. Well, amen. Keep asking for more revelation of His Love to you. It is the forerunner to *loving Him* (1 John 4:19). In a soon coming book, *all i want is JESUS! – Vol.1,* I will give you 13 short chapters on The Love of God...*all i want is HIS LOVE!*

That we might be filled with all the fullness of God.

Now listen. Being *filled with all the fullness of God* is a matter of being filled with Holy Spirit. Go back and re-read ch. 20. Uncomplicated. *Be being filled* are Holy Spirit's instructions in Ephesians 5:18. Uncomplicated.

> And be not drunk with wine, wherein is excess, but be filled with the Spirit.

And Holy Spirit CAN reveal to us that knowledge of Christ's Love! And His filling!

Chapter 28

The Principle of Grace

Now to him that worketh is the reward
not reckoned of grace, but of debt.
Romans 4:4

Hidden (a mystery to be sure!) amongst these simple words is the clear description separating *our works* and the *work of God*. *Our works* may pay for some debt, but none of which in God's realm can we ever pay in full. *God's works* are *His grace*. *His grace* has paid *in full* whatever needed to be paid.

God tells us in John 1 that Jesus came and dwelt among the people *full of grace and truth.* And, that *of His fullness have all we received, and grace for grace.* God always acts on the *principle of grace*. That is Him. He does the works…THAT is *His grace*. We don't deserve anything we get from Him, but He does the doing.

Two things I have never been able to understand since I became a Christian:
1. why do so few really not know what *grace* truthfully is?
2. how so few are recognizing the *grace of God* as a reality in their day to day living. This is not intended to be an unknown teaching, yet so many seem to miss it as such. Of course, an erroneous definition leads to an erroneous path/end.

While we are here, look at verse 3 in Romans chapter 4:
> For what saith the scripture? Abraham believed God,
> and it was counted unto him for righteousness.

That is the great illustration of verse 4. *Grace* is God *working*, when we *believe*, and we get righteousness *counted* unto us, for us. What a deal! In terms of our work or effort, none. In terms of our believing, yes! Yet, in so many aspects of life, believing seems impossible for so many.

Spiritual Life is always a situation of His *grace* instead of our *works*. Beware of any person who wants to put some work upon you to make an impression for God. Jesus told us that most of these folks don't do half of what they tell you that you must do.

> Then spake Jesus to the multitude, and to his disciples, Saying, The scribes and the Pharisees sit in Moses' seat: All therefore whatsoever they bid you observe, that observe and do; but do not ye after their works: for they say, and do not…But all their works they do for to be seen of men… Matthew 23:1-3, 5

Jesus laid the *works* argument of the Pharisees to rest, didn't He? Jesus doesn't say the things taught in Scripture are not to be done, but to not depend on our *works* when we should depend on *His*. And we are not to do *works* to try and impress God or people.

Listen. A reward is awarded for doing some *work*. Someone who thinks they can *work* their way into Heaven or for some benefit here on earth is looking for that *reward*. *Grace* is a *gift*, not a *reward*. God gifts us with *His grace* (His *doing*) because He *loves*, not because *we work*.

I love that which Michael Wells, Steve McVey, Watchman Nee, Bill Gothard, Jerry Bridges, Ian Thomas, Spiros Zodhiates, and Hannah Whitall Smith have described for us just what God wants to *do* instead of His expecting *us to do*.

> At my point of need, God is everything to me that I thought He was not. Michael Wells

> God does it all. It is the Divine enablement of Christ's Life in a Believer that enables us to be/do all that Christ intends for us to be/do…yet it is Him doing it, not us. Steve McVey

> Grace means that God does something for me. Watchman Nee

> Grace is God's dynamic power given to Christians to accomplish God's will. Bill Gothard

Grace is God's divine enablement through the power of His Holy Spirit. Jerry Bridges

Grace provides…faith appropriates. Ian Thomas

Charisma (grace) is the instantaneous enablement of the Holy Spirit in the life of any believer to exercise a gift for the edification of others. Spiros Zodhiates

Grace is the unhindered, wondrous, boundless love of God, poured out upon us in an infinite variety of ways by His measureless heart of love. To grow in grace means being planted in the very heart of this Divine love, to put ourselves in His hands and leave it with Him. Hannah Whitall Smith

Grace is simply the *Life of Christ* that dwells in our earthsuit. Christ wants to Live *His Life* through our earthsuit just as God the Father Lived *His Life* through the earthsuit of Christ. WOW! What a plan by Almighty God to give us *His Life* to *Live Life as a Christian*…instead of our struggling to do so in the *flesh*.

This is the *Principle of Grace*. The actual *principle* in *action* is what we get to enjoy day after day when we have learned to *know* this principle, *believe* God's Truth, *trust* His Truth, *abandon* self to Christ, and *receive* His Life as our Life. The *action* comes in the next chapter!

And, these are great Truths to enjoy Christ's Life by! The Principle of Grace in our Life.

Chapter 29

The Practice of Grace

*And that ye put on the new man, which after God
is created in righteousness and true holiness.*
Ephesians 4:24

Ok, we closed out the previous chapter on the *principle of grace* with an outline of this *practice of grace*. Here it is again: learn to *know* the principle of *grace, believe* God's Truth, *trust* His Truth, *abandon* self to Christ, and *receive* His Life as our Life. This is what is called the *Grace Life*. This is the *New Man* in action.

The context of Paul's writing here is the *putting off of the old man* and the *putting on of the New Man*. This is simply where Believers recognize who we used to be, and don't want any of that life…and we sure do want to know who we now are, and want all of it we can get. Again I remind us that the Life of this *New Man* is Christ. And it is His Life Lived (His Grace) through our earthsuit that yields the *practice of grace* we are speaking about in this chapter.

Now listen, when we go to God and abandon *self*, He will negate the *old man* and activate all of the *New Man* through our earthsuit. We can't do this in our fleshly actions. It just doesn't work that way. Trying to not be the *old man*, and trying to be the *New Man*, is a formula for failure. That is a proven fact millions of times by Saints over the ages. God has to do this through us, or Christ's Life will not be experienced. THAT is one of the greatest mysteries (parables, allegories) of Christianity.

We know it is good to have an outline for anything. However, we also know that an outline is NOT action. The outline is a *guide* to action. So, let's first look at the *action* of the *practice of grace*, the *Grace Life*, then we can come back and think about how to *put it into practice*. The first thing we notice is God telling us in our text verse that we are to *put on the New Man*. Be sure you remember that this is not work that *we* do, but something we *appropriate*. To *appropriate* is to take (something/someone) for one's own use, and in the case of Christians we are taking Someone Who has been *given* to us. ALL actions in the Life of a Christian are to be actions of Holy Spirit *given to us* in our New Birth. Be sure you see where God said this *New Man* (us, the New Birth, New Creation) was/is *created in righteousness and true holiness after God*. It is a done deal, by God Himself *(His creation)*, not of us. Done. It does not need to be our doing. Just needs to be *appropriated*. Hallelujah! Our *New Man* has been created in righteousness and true holiness. That's us!

The question we can ask at this time is this: *what does this New Man look like?* Ok, we turn back to Ephesians 4…

> That ye put off concerning the former conversation *(conversation means lifestyle)* the old man *(the old man was the Sinner you used to be)*, which is corrupt according to deceitful lusts; and be renewed in the spirit of your mind *(the Spirit of your mind is the new Christ's Mind you were given at the New Birth…be in the New Mind)*; And that ye put on the new man, which after God is created in righteousness and true holiness. Wherefore putting away lying, speak every man truth with his neighbor: for we are members one of another. Be ye angry, and sin not: let not the sun go down on your wrath: Neither give place to the devil. Let him who stole steal no more: but rather let him labor, working with his hands the thing which is good, that he may have to give to him that needeth. Let no corrupt communication proceed out of your mouth, but that which is good to the use of edifying, that it may minister grace unto the hearers. And grieve not the Holy Spirit of God, whereby ye are sealed unto the day of redemption. Let all bitterness, and wrath, and anger, and clamour, and evil speaking, be put away from you, with all malice: And be ye kind one to another, tender-hearted, forgiving one another, even as God for Christ's sake hath forgiven you. 4:22-32

Verses 25 through 32 are Christ Living out of our earthsuit! And verses 22-23 connect with Philippians 1:27, *italicized words in parentheses my explanation…*

> Only let your conversation *(lifestyle)* be as it becometh the gospel of Christ: that whether I come and see you, or else be absent, I may hear of your affairs, that ye stand fast in one spirit *(Holy Spirit)*, with one mind *(the Mind of Christ)* striving together for the faith of the gospel.

Wow! What a connection to the *practice of grace* and the Holy Spirit/Soul of Christ in Believers!

Ok, we have what the *action* looks like in real life. How do we *appropriate* (put into practice) the action. Well, we have learned the *principle* and have seen the *action* of the *principle*. All of this has pointed us to Jesus Christ and what He will do for us. Enter a huge question: *will we believe and trust God's Truth?* Will we believe that every seeming instruction for something our *New Man* is supposed to do is truthfully an instruction from God to Holy Spirit in us to do the doing? HE is our *New Man* in our earthsuit; not some makeover, do-over, renovation of our *old man*. Our answer decides for us whether we will *abandon* self to Christ. IF we *believe and trust God,* then we will *abandon* our *self* to Christ. *Self* is that residue of the *old man,* the *old soul (old mind, old emotions, old will, old heart),* still in all Saints after the New Birth. (see the trichotomy diagrams in ch. 8 and get this settled in your New Mind. Believe all you really are as a Saint). The only thing left is to *receive* Christ's Life as our Life.

It is in the *abandoning* that many sincere Believers get hung up. *Yield* is a word many can probably understand and relate to. In essence, the two are the same, EXCEPT in *yielding* some take that to mean they *give up*, stop, get off the *playing field*. To *abandon* is to *stay in the game* but do so by allowing Holy Spirit in us to become us, our Life. And this is what God wants us to do. Let Him Live His Life through us. But our earthsuit is *in the game*, not *sitting on the bench out of play*. All Spiritual effort is to be done by Christ. Now listen, here is the *key,* we simply *trust* Him to do that.

Let me remind you I like to use a simple prayer, or statement to God like this: *Holy Spirit, make known to me, make experiential to me, all that Christ is in me. Holy Spirit, I choose to allow You to occupy the whole of my personality, my earthsuit, my being, with the adequacy of Christ. And I trust You to do so and thank You that You will.* At that point, I have *abandoned* self to God and *trusted* Him to be Living His Life through me. Before you say that sounds too easy, or that can't work...try it. Having difficulty getting rid of something in your life? Try it. Having difficulty doing something Spiritually that you would like to do? Try it. Give God the time and the opportunity to prove His Truth to you.

This last *step* is called *receiving*. Whether you have been aware of it, or not, you have already done this for one Spiritual Truth...being Born Again. Look at God's Word about being Born Again:

> He came unto his own, and His own received Him not.
> But as many as received Him, to them gave He power to
> become the sons of God, even to them that believe on
> His name. John 1:11-12

How about that! Verse 12, to those who *believe* on His Name (Jesus) and *receive* Him, He gives the power to be *Born Again* as a child of God. Remember ch. 14? *Believe* – Greek: *pisteuo,* meaning to believe in, give credit to, be persuaded. *Received* – Greek: *lambano*, meaning to take in, grab hold of. That is, to take it as your own...to *own it*. That is what really *trusting in Jesus Christ to be my Savior* means. And when you did that, you *lambano*'d Christ.

However, now listen! It is interesting, and something you need to know for yourself as well as to tell others: *received* in John 1:11 is from a totally different Greek word with a completely different meaning, *paralambano*, to receive near, but NOT take in...to associate with someone, perhaps learn of, but NOT become one with. BIG DIFFERENCE! That is why the Bible tells us we are to make sure we have *lambano*'d Christ, and NOT *paralambano*'d Him. Well, amen.

Ok, let's get back to this *Practice of Grace* issue. All the Spiritual things mentioned in 4:22-32 and elsewhere in the Bible will become a part of our Life IF we have let Holy Spirit's Life become *our* Life. This is putting *His Grace* into *practice*. This is the *putting on of the New Man*.

Growing in grace (see ch.48) is an instruction for us (2 Peter 3:18) to simply *allow* more of Holy Spirit's Life through our earthsuit. More of Him, less of *me* (*self, residue of old man*). The battles between the two souls (2 minds, 2 sets of emotions, 2 wills, 2 *hearts*) get fewer and fewer as you abandon to Holy Spirit and His Life. In fact, you will *grow in His Grace* to the point that much of what you used to struggle with has *fallen off* (as my friend, Michael Wells, put it), and your days will be full of peace, comfort, and joy without any of the consternations, complications, and confusion you might sometimes face today.

And His Grace will live His Life through us every moment we are abandoned to Him.

Chapter 30

Abandoned to God

> I beseech you therefore, brethren, by the mercies of God,
> that ye present your bodies a living sacrifice, holy,
> acceptable unto God, which is your reasonable service.
> And be not conformed to this world: but be ye
> transformed by the renewing of your mind,
> that ye may prove what is that good, and
> acceptable, and perfect will of God.
> Romans 12:1-2

By now you have seen that I like to repeat something over and over. This is not to say that I think you didn't *get it* the first or second time, but that repetition *confirms* and *reinforces* what is already there. You and I have learned that from sports or a lot of other different ways, haven't we! It's not practice that makes perfect (complete), but *correct* practice makes *correct perfect/completion*. So, let's take another look at being *abandoned*.

It is the correct definitions of Scriptural words that make the difference whether we know what God has truthfully said, or not. *Abandoned* is not a Scriptural word. It is not found anywhere in the Holy Scriptures. It is, however, a Scriptural concept. And that concept dates back to 1300 A. D. or before: *to give up control to someone*. One Scriptural word most closely related would be *wait*. To *wait* on the Lord can be to acknowledge that God is our Master, and we are one of His bond-slaves, choosing to do His bidding.

One of the greatest mysteries of God of all time is that we as Saints are truthfully not ourselves. Our original *old man* was crucified. Removed. Replaced by our New Man, Who is Christ. We have been *bought with a price*, yes, BUT...*we are a New Creation (ch.7)*. A New Creation is something New, not the Old revamped. Therefore, the new us has a capability that those who are not Saints of God do not have. Holy Spirit in us gives us His Life. Our choice must be to *abandon*, or yield, our earthsuit and our *self*, the *old soul* still in us, to God in *perfect (complete) abandonment* to God for His Life to be Lived through our earthsuit.

Do I still choose to physically brush my teeth without His having to do it? Yes. Do I still choose to eat and drink to nourish my physical earthsuit without His having to do it? Yes. These are physical things that are not really all that Spiritual, but can have Spiritual implications…in which I then do have to *abandon* to Him for control on some of these issues.

Ok, let us look at some of the key words in Romans 12:1 to get a fuller meaning, dissecting this verse in context of the Grace Life of Saints:

Bodies – our earthsuit, the physical *body* of Saints on earth, housing Holy Spirit and two souls (Christ's Soul given by God at our Spiritual birth and the natural soul, given to us at our physical birth).

Living sacrifice – every Saint's *old life* has already been crucified at the New Birth, and there is no call in Scripture for a Saint to make another sacrifice. That which has been crucified was replaced with Holy Spirit, the Life of Christ. We may not *see* Him, or *feel* Him, but His Life is now *our* Life. Holy Spirit is our *living sacrifice*. Every day on earth the New Creation is Living out of that original sacrifice (*zao thusia*). Galatians 2:20 (ch.17) is a prime example of this Truth.

Holy – the life of every Saint is the Life of Christ. Colossians 3:4 (ch.21) is God's statement to that fact. That makes *our* Life *Holy*. *We are Holy* because of His Life being our Life, not because of any other actions. When God looks at a Saint, He sees a *Holy Life*. As Believers, you and I are *holy*.

Acceptable to God – this follows as a given since it is Christ's Life that is *acceptable*. That is how God tells us that *we* are *accepted in the beloved* in Ephesians 1:7.

Now, here is where the words gets critical…

Reasonable service – *logikos latreia*, the reasonable service or worship, is to be understood as that service or worship to God which implies intelligent meditation or reflection. Worship is a better idea of what God speaks of when telling us to *abandon to Him*. Worship is to bow before

God, showing His *worth* to us, giving Him our adoring acknowledgement as *GOD*.

To present our earthsuit to God is to *abandon to Him* for Him to Live His Life through us. It has always been God's intention for this. That's *worship*. Showing His *worth-ship*.

Ok, let us now look at 12:2 for a fuller meaning in context of Christ's Grace Life in Saints:

Transformed – *metamorphoo*, also used in Matthew 17:2 and Mark 9:2, the miracle of transformation from an earthly form into a Supernatural. This Truth is important here. This is not about physical changes, but Supernatural Spiritual changes.

Renewing – *anakainosis*, qualitatively new. Here Holy Spirit moves the Apostle Paul to use the New *Mind of Christ* Believers have. The Supernatural (God's transformation, *metamorphoo*) creation in Believers speaks of using only the Supernatural *Mind of Christ*. This is not speaking of trying to enhance in any way the *natural* mind. Believers should never use the *natural* mind.

These two verses are excellent examples of the *parabolic* teaching of God that the *natural* mind (of lost persons and Believers living in the wrong mind) will not grasp nor understand, and miss out on the Life of Christ in the earthsuit.

Acceptable – *euarestos*, that which God wills and recognizes. It is very important to know that this writing is speaking of only that which God wills (His Heart on something) and recognizes (accepts). Hence the closing statement, *perfect will of God*.

Perfect – *teleios*, God's perfection which is absolute (humankind's is relative). Something/someone is *teleios* in God's eyes when it/he has attained the goal which has been set by God for it/him.

Let me close with two things again needing to be totally emphasized: 1. Life as a Christian is *living from*, not *living to*. We do not *live to* get something that has already been *given* to us. 2. Every word, phrase, sentence, verse, chapter in Scripture is parabolic in nature because God is speaking Spiritually to His Children (Saints, Believers) and not physically. Wrong awareness leads to wrong understanding, which leads to wrong acknowledgement, which leads to *wrong living*. Far too many

Saints are living from the *flesh* instead of enjoying Christ's Life in their earthsuit by *abandoning* to Him, and end up frustrated because it is not working out for them.

Abandonment to God always produces His Life which is the victorious, overcoming Life of Saints!

Chapter 31

Holy Spirit Power Alive In Us

> But if the Spirit of Him that raised up Jesus from the dead
> dwell in you, He that raised up Christ from the dead
> shall also quicken your mortal bodies by His Spirit
> that dwelleth in you.
> Romans 8:11

There are a few Scriptural verses that will bring back some distinct memories of your years here on earth. Romans 8:11 is one of those for me.

I don't remember exactly where I was (although it must have been at Sagemont Church in Houston sometime in 1980) when I first saw this verse, but I do remember the shock and the thrill of God revealing to me that Holy Spirit was alive and well and indwelling my earthsuit as a Saint! Wow! Isn't that an incredible thought and realization? That made me want to take off my shoes and run around the room clapping the soles together and start shouting, "Glory to God! Hallelujah!"

Let me include a few more verses in chapter 8 before I give you more of my thoughts of why this is a great Life Verse:

> For if ye live after the flesh, ye shall die: but if ye through the Spirit do mortify the deeds of the body, ye shall live. For as many as are led by the Spirit of God, they are the sons of God. For ye have not received the spirit of bondage again to fear; but ye have received the Spirit of adoption, whereby we cry, Abba, Father. The Spirit itself beareth witness with our spirit, that we are the children of God: And if children, then heirs; heirs of God, and joint-heirs with Christ; if so be that we suffer with him, that we may be also glorified together. Romans 8:13-17

Incredible. Each verse giving us such profound Truth and electrifying benefits of being a Child of God. Amen!

So, look back at our text verse for a moment. God raised up Jesus from the dead. Stop right there. This is one of the several verses that mention God and Jesus and Holy Spirit in the same verse, the Trinity. Keep in mind that God is Jesus Christ in an earthsuit, and Jesus Christ in an earthsuit is God. God Himself as Holy Spirit raised Jesus Christ (God) from the dead. This is a test of a Saint being able to discern this very important Truth. Anyone who does not believe that Jesus is God (and vice versa) needs to come to that revelation. It is one thing to have never been presented with this Truth, but upon hearing or reading this, Holy Spirit will confirm this Truth to a Born Again Saint so that there is no unbelief or confusion about this Truth.

But now listen! This same Holy Spirit, Who indwells us Saints, has the power to *raise someone from the physically dead*. That was Jesus when He was crucified and buried. That's US at our physical death. OK. That's a good start. But then, God tells us that IF He dwells in us, AND HE DOES, He shall *quicken our mortal body* (that's our earthsuit that contains Holy Spirit and our two souls) right here in our time on the earth. It takes the *Mind of Christ* to keep up with this, doesn't it! I'm loving it, aren't you?

But how does this last thing happen? He actually wants to Live His Life through our earthsuit, remember? So, His *quickening of our earthsuit* is easy for Him when we are abandoned to Him, and His Life and control. Well, I'll be.

Now, who said *living the Christian life is difficult?* Actually it is, in the *flesh*. But that is because of a Saint trying to do the impossible. Only the Lord Jesus Christ (God come in an earthsuit, with Holy Spirit quickening His earthsuit, Who knew NO sin) has ever Lived the Life some call *the Christian life*. His Life was a perfect Life, available to all Saints with the Truth of Romans 8:11. Do you want to know something…there is no such thing as *the Christian life*, someone's description of a lifestyle to try and obtain, a set of rules to keep, trying to being perfect. *Life as a Christian*, however, for a Saint is not difficult, but easy, with Christ doing the Living by Holy Spirit doing the quickening. Well, amen.

Let me encourage you to delve into those other 5 verses and let Holy Spirit show you so much more that is yours as a Saint simply from His indwelling you. Especially the words that speak of *through the Spirit, by the Spirit, beareth witness, and glorified together.* But for now, let it suffice for us to know that we ARE children of God and heirs to ALL He is and has.

And Holy Spirit will confirm all that while He is quickening your mortal body with His power!

Chapter 32

Exceeding Abundantly

> Now unto Him that is able to do exceeding abundantly above
> all that we ask or think, according to the power that worketh in us,
> Unto Him be glory in all the church by Christ Jesus
> throughout all ages, world without end. Amen.
> Ephesians 3:20-21

Barbara might have a hissy fit if I didn't include these verses as some of our most favorite Life Verses. I think verse 20 is her most favorite verse of all in the Holy Scriptures. But I love it also!

Think about the awesome power that is spoken of in the first few words of verse 20...*able to do exceeding abundantly above all that we ask or think*. God is able. There is nothing He cannot do. In fact, how could any Saint EVER think there might be something God couldn't do? We believe Genesis 1 and 2, don't we? God created the heaven and the earth, and everything dwelling therein, including the first two human beings. Created. Made all those and them from nothing. Are you kidding me that some Saints do not believe *all things are possible with God?!?*

But listen, not only is God *able* but He can do *exceeding abundantly above* anything and all we *ask* or *think*. Wow! That's a trip. When we start Living in the *Mind of Christ* and begin to get into the *Will* and *Heart* of Christ, not only are there NO LIMITS to where that can take us, but there are NO LIMITS to where HE might want to take us, or may take us. Oh, how we limit God by living so much of our time out of our *finite natural mind* in our *old soul*. That is the mind that limits God. That is the mind that hinders the *exceeding abundantly* from becoming reality. We may never know what those areas in the *outer limits* are simply because we have the tendency to spend more time with the *finite natural mind* than in the *infinite Mind of Christ*.

But, look, God goes on to tell us we are back in Romans 8:11 territory (Holy Spirit power to raise Jesus from the dead territory)! This Holy Spirit and His power dwelling IN us is the power *that worketh in us* whereby He (God) is ABLE to do the *exceeding abundantly above all that we ask or think* through us.

This is not a free ticket to go wherever we want to go at any time we want to go.
This is not a free ticket out of jail anytime we want it.
This is not a free gift of anything and everything we want at any time we want whatever.
This is not a free power to make anything happen we want to happen.
This is a recognition that *all that we ask or think* must be in the *Will* of God. In His *Heart* on anything. Yet, still this is tremendous when we stop and meditate on this. And this is reality moreso when we *ask* or *think* in the Spiritual realm than the physical realm. God is more into the Spiritual realm than He is the physical, *although* He does travel in the physical a whole bunch.

So, let us put this into perspective. First, we need to *ask* or *think* more in the Spiritual realm. Next, we need to be *asking* and *thinking* that God wants to do *exceeding abundantly* some Spiritual work with the *power that worketh in us*. And, He wants us to get to be a part of all this because He is using Holy Spirit indwelling us. There is a verse that Jesus gave hint to this very Truth:
> Verily, verily, I say unto you, He that believeth on Me,
> the works that I do shall he do also; and greater works
> than these shall he do; because I go unto my Father.
> John 14:12

Talk about a parabolic teaching! How many Saints *get* this statement from Jesus, much less the Lost having no clue whatsoever! But His words are Truth and Life. His words are testimony to two things we must grasp: one, Saints (Believers who have believed, *pisteuo*...a moral commitment) will *do the works Jesus did*, only it is not the physical Saint but the Spiritual Saint (with Holy Spirit being the One Who is doing the works), and two, *greater works* being done involves most Saints having more time than Jesus was on earth for Holy Spirit to do *greater works*.

The Greek translated *greater* in English is *meizon,* more. Not greater in the sense of something more magnificent than feeding 5,000 or raising someone from the dead, but in number/amount of works. Do you see WHY I emphasize knowing the Greek words behind the English translation and our considering Scripture with the *Mind of Christ* (His eyes, His ears, His thoughts and knowledge)?

Well it is easy to see why Holy Spirit led the Apostle Paul to close the chapter with these words in verse 21…*Unto God be glory* (naturally, it is His glory that He will not share with just anyone…but mainly because it is Him doing the work!) *in the body of Christ* (that is what the true church is) *by Christ* Jesus (*by*, the Greek *en*, meaning *resting in Christ's work*, as the One doing it) *throughout all ages* (all generations), *world without end* (or, until this world comes to an end)… *Amen.*

And God will see that He is glorified by His power being shown through His Saints!

Chapter 33

Do All Things

*I can do all things through Christ
which strengtheneth me.
Philippians 4:13*

This might well be the *fight song* of the *Works Team*. But, there is something sad about this…I hardly ever hear them singing it! It's no wonder. Anyone on the *Works Team* has tried over and over and over to *do all things* and come up tired and empty, wondering how this supposed *strength of Christ* didn't work. The *Works Team*'s efforts don't work. How ironic is that!

Unfortunately, the misleading translation and parabolic nature of this verse does much to throw so many into the *flesh life (works, Works Team)*. Taking the instruction to mean this is something *we do*, albeit in the *strength of Christ*, is never what God intended for *Life as a Christian* to be. So, how does this and similar verses tend to be misunderstood and lead Believers into an unattainable life, as well as prove to Unbelievers that *the Christian life* leads only to despair and hypocrisy? Parabolism. Parabolic teaching. And the misleading translation of one word.

This verse is like all other *do* verses. When anyone does not know, or remember, and adhere to Truth that any teaching seen as landing at the individual's feet and telling the individual what he/she must do is parabolic teaching, they are headed for defeat. What is really sad in this verse is there is *one critical word* that is misunderstood because the English translations make it appear to be one thing when the Greek word correctly translated says something different. And that one misunderstanding leads many to get on the wrong team.

That word is the English *through*. The Greek *en* (same word as in the previous chapter) has a primary meaning of *rest in any place, thing,* and in this case *person*. Its use implies *in* or *remaining in*. Now listen, Living in the

Mind of Christ I immediately think how this meaning takes me to John 15 and the word *abiding*. With the fundamental picture of Jesus being *the Vine* and we are *branches* in *the Vine*, branches do nothing apart from what the vine feeds through the branch. We can never forget that fundamental Truth.

So many take the English *through* and live like it is them living and doing simply because they are a Christian and it's the Christian thing to do, or they can do with Christ's help, or they can do just from being a part of the Family of God. The problem for most begins with the parabolic *I can do*. Jesus said in John 15:5, *we can do nothing, apart from Him*, actually meaning His doing the doing, vine/branches. The meaning of that verse is lost when Saints move from the Vine/branch picture to just them living life with a little help from Christ.

Ok, we have the verse now telling us, *all things can be done by the indwelling Holy Spirit through our earthsuit even though it will appear that we are the ones doing it.* This is always the Truth behind God's parabolic teaching to His Saints. It is never *us* that accomplishes the Spiritual. It is always *Holy Spirit/Jesus/God*. Which is testimony of *who we are in Christ* and *who Christ is in us.*

Before we leave this chapter, let me give an illustration and application of this Truth from another passage: Ephesians 3:8-16...*italicized words my emphasis.*

> Unto me, who am less than the least of all saints, is this *grace* given, that I should preach among the Gentiles the unsearchable riches of Christ; And to make all men see what is the fellowship of the mystery, which from the beginning of the world hath been hid in God, who created all things *by* Jesus Christ: To the intent that now unto the principalities and powers in heavenly places might be known by the church the manifold wisdom of God, According to the eternal purpose which he purposed *in* Christ Jesus our Lord: *In* whom we have boldness and access with confidence *by the faith of him.* Wherefore I desire that ye faint not at my tribulations for you, which is your glory. For this cause I bow my knees unto the Father of our Lord Jesus Christ, *Of* whom the whole family in heaven and earth is named. That he

> would grant you, according to the riches of his glory, to
> be strengthened with might *by* his Spirit *in* the inner man.

What a powerful testimony of what *grace* truthfully is, and how that works out *in* our earthsuit *by His Spirit in the* (our) *inner man*. Remember, *grace* is *God doing something through us*. And how beautiful this is in connection with John 14:12,

> Verily, verily, I say unto you, He that believeth on me,
> the works that I do shall he do also; and greater works
> than these shall he do; because I go unto my Father.

First of all, *verily* is a word that is probably better understood as *truly*. But, this verse we spoke of back in Chapter 32. The *greater* works being numerically, not of superiority. Still, *all the works* are of God's doing, not a Saint's. Well, amen.

And Christ in us CAN do ALL things He purposes to do in His will.

Chapter 34

Blessed With All Spiritual Blessings

*Blessed be the God and Father of our Lord Jesus Christ,
who hath blessed us with all spiritual blessings
in heavenly places in Christ.
Ephesians 1:3*

Don't let the *heavenly places* fool you, or get you to thinking none of this applies to life on earth. It all does. God is omnipresent, everywhere all the time (only Believers can *believe* that). The New Testament makes it clear that WE are in the heavenlies *and* here on earth all because of Him in us. How does that grab you?!?

Two things are important here: Father God has blessed us with ALL Spiritual blessings, and they are given to us IN CHRIST. We started thinking about that back in chapter 24 with this same verse. Then followed with the next 11 verses. Yet we were looking at some of the particulars of what it is to BE IN CHRIST. Here, we will look solely at the point of *blessed us with all spiritual blessings*. That is Truth we must recognize, believe, trust in, and receive so that we don't get sidetracked into thinking *we* have much to do with Spiritual blessings, of which too many start praising self or others instead of praising God.

So, let's digest 4 words. *Blessed. Blessings. Spiritual. Heavenly.* These are the mainstays of this great Truth expressed here. The English word *blessed* appears twice in the verse. But, there are two different Greek words translated *blessed*. In the first appearance, the first word of the verse, *eulogetos* is the Greek word, derived from *eulogeo* which is the root Greek word of both appearances. *Eulogia* is the second Greek word translated in *hath blessed us*. Is there any difference? Slightly. *Eulogetos* speaks of one to be well spoken of (in this case, God the Father). *Eulogia* speaks of a good word or action of God. Therefore, we Believers have received a good word or action of God, who is One to be well spoken of. It is good for us to remember that it is Almighty God who has taken action here *to* us, *in* us, *for* us…*all spiritual blessings.* When God has blessed us with ALL spiritual blessings, we need to sit up and take notice!

OK, *all* means all. Everything that could be included. There is truthfully no limit to His Spiritual blessings. (remember, I like to capitalize a word that is directly related to, or inclusive of, Him). It is a huge matter to grasp the totality of His blessings. Whenever we take the focus off what God has done for us and put the focus on what we need to do for God, or what we need to do to get something from God, we move from Christianity to some man-made religion. Bad move! This is what plagues most Christians (and therefore, churches) today. The world is not impressed with ANY man-made religion. The world has its own man-made religion, *humanism*. And since their religion teaches that *they* are their own *god*, they think they are superior to us "plain humans." (Maybe we should ask them how that is working out for them!). The arguments for each are endless and neither side wins. But, listen! THE WORLD HAS NOTHING TO COMPETE WITH TRUTHFUL CHRISTIANITY. It has no god that can compete with Almighty God! So, we must stick with God and His Truth and not deviate one iota.

Once more, I think the Holy Scriptures translators have done a huge disservice (to put it mildly) by not putting certain specific words with a capital letter at the first. This leads to a lack of recognition of the source (or, Source), a lack of importance or dramatic impact, often a misunderstanding of *who* one is in a verse, etc., etc., etc. All kinds of Scriptural implications are missing when we do not give due recognition to God or His manifestations.

> Let me insert something to emphasize the importance of what I am saying. The Holy Scriptures tell us of more than one spirit in this world. Holy Spirit and all *other spirits*. In fact, for all *non-judgers* in the church (or, outside the church), God tells us in *1 John 4:1,* "Beloved, believe not every spirit, but try the spirits whether they are of God…" Tell me how anyone can "try the spirits whether they are of God" without *judging*. We can't. So, it is imperative to KNOW Whose *Spirit* or *Spiritual blessing* is being mentioned.

Therefore, *Spiritual* in verse 3 with a capital *S* marks the blessings as more than just *a blessing*, or from just *a spirit*. As we saw in vs. 4-14, those *blessings* are of dramatic impact in every Christian's Life (Christ's LIFE). Verse 3 sets the table for ALL the *Spiritual blessings* that Paul writes about in Ephesians, as well as all his writings. When we see *love, joy, peace, faith, long-suffering, meekness, temperance, gentleness, justification, sanctification, Eternal Life*, and on and on…we should be alert to each of these being a *gift*, a *Spiritual blessing* from God to us, blessings which only Christians enjoy. Verse 3 is a powerful Life Verse.

Now, one more thing: *heavenly*. *Heavenly places*, to be exact and complete…oh, *in Christ*. Alright Paul, what is Holy Spirit saying through you to close out this important verse? Very simply, God has *blessed* us with all of His *Spiritual blessings* in Heaven, and differentiates them from any earthly blessings that could be from someone other than God. Once again, this emphasizes to Believers the great importance of Living in the *heavenlies* instead of on the earth. Keeping everything in life here on earth in a *heavenly perspective* and *context* enables us to maintain our fellowship with the Trinity as He desires.

Well, amen.

Living in heavenly places brings all Spiritual blessings to LIFE!

Chapter 35

Fruit of Holy Spirit

> But the fruit of the Spirit is love, joy, peace, long-suffering,
> gentleness, goodness, faith, meekness, temperance:
> against such there is no law.
> Galatians 5:22-23

These are two uncomplicated verses tucked away in a chapter speaking of the struggle between a Christian's *flesh* and the *Spiritual Being* that we really are. These verses get quoted a lot. And many call the *Fruit* the *fruits*, but it is important to know Holy Spirit meant the singular, not the plural…speaking of each one individually.

The reason is uncomplicated. God is telling us what is His nature, not that which He grows or generates. Remember? *IS* means *equals*. Same as. Same thing. God's *Love* cannot be separated from God. God's *Faith* cannot be separated from God. The same holds for every other *Fruit* listed here. Each Fruit is Him.

What is most beautiful is that this is a picture of *who we are* in Christ, and *Who He wants to be* through our earthsuit. These *Fruit* are a part of *our Being*, and we experience and enjoy them (Him) when we are *abandoned* to Christ and there is *no quenching* of Holy Spirit. That is incredible news. Again, these are not *fruits* that we have to try and obtain. Each is a *gift* to us as children of God. Listen, in gardening, fruit comes from the flow of life from the vine through the branch. Can you picture this Spiritually? Jesus (the Vine) with His Life flowing through us (His branches) yields His *Fruit*. Him. Beautiful. Not a struggle or battle on our part, but a *receiving* through our *believing and trusting*.

A big issue for us is to know more of Christ that is available to us, and to experience all of *His Fruit* day after day. Think about each one and how wonderful it is to experience these. All of these are intended to be a manifestation of the *Grace of God* in His Saints.

Notice the first three focus on an inward Being, that which makes our innermost Being so full of His grace. I have asked a question of multitudes and almost all give close to the same answer. *"Name me one thing you would love for God to provide to your innermost Being."* I almost always get one of the first three! Then the next three speak of dispositions we would most want to have in our interaction with other people, especially loved ones and other Saints. And, finally, that last three speak of dispositions we most want to enjoy in our own walk. God, in His infinite wisdom and infinite Being, has GIVEN every Saint all of Himself that we possess and can experience, and enjoy, each and every day as we live a Spirit-filled Life, His Life, the Grace Life.

Love – (in a coming book, *all i want is Jesus! – vol. 1,* I write 13 chapters on the *Love of God*) For now, just know that True Love is God manifested to a person and giving that person what they need, not necessarily what they want. All else is counterfeit. That person can be you and I.

Joy – (this is coming in *all i want is Jesus! – vol. 2*) It really is comforting to know the huge difference between *Joy*, as part of and a gift of God Himself, and *happiness*, which the world gives with things and events, etc. Nothing the world can offer compares with the *Joy of the Lord*, no matter the circumstances or the time.

Peace – (coming in *all i want is Jesus! – vol. 2* also) Check out chapter 40 in this book for more right now.

Longsuffering – Now here is a word most just pass over when reading this verse! Isn't it amazing this grace appears right after the first three which are more like the results of communion with God and not in combat with the world. We need *Longsuffering* when dealing with events or others. And so the *Life of God (Holy Spirit flowing through us)* yields the power to *bear all things*, to face harsh treatment, rudeness, even injustice or just someone being unkind and our Spiritual Heart shows sweetness and Love through whatever comes our way.

Gentleness – Christ's Life gives us the disposition to be soft-spoken, kind, and even-tempered in our interaction with all others. 2 Timothy 2:24 tells us to *"be gentle unto all men…patient"* among other things. This is *Fruit of Holy Spirit* at its finest shown to another.

Goodness – This *Fruit* is being virtuous, benevolent, generous, but the Apostle Paul used a Greek word that specifically highlights *character* *energized* as *active good* that can even be shown in rebuking, or correcting, or chastising someone. An example is in Matthew 21:13 where Jesus showed *goodness* when He showed righteous indignation in the temple to those money-changers and declared, *"It is written, My house shall be called the house of prayer; but ye have made it a den of thieves."* The Greek here makes clear and desirable what our English idea causes misunderstanding to most.

Faith – In chapters 15-18 I have given detailed explanations and illustrations on what Christ's *Faith* is & how Christ's *Faith* becomes real in us, *our* Faith.

Meekness – Most consider this to be a disposition balanced in tempers and passions (Aristotle said this was a grace that stands between two extremes – uncontrolled, unjustified anger and not becoming angry at all no matter what takes place around you), showing no revenge, indulgent, even weakness…however, Jesus never showed any weakness. Our Lord showed that this *Fruit* was not really any outward expression of feeling, but an *inward grace* of His Soul exhibiting *calmness*.

Temperance – This disposition of Holy Spirit speaks of being self-controlled, especially in a moderate way of the indulgences of appetites and passions. Self-control is a great *Fruit* of Holy Spirit for every Christian in a world where few have this grace. Peter tells us it is one of eight graces of God, if they abound in us, that will guarantee to make us *"neither barren or unfruitful in the knowledge of our Lord Jesus Christ" (2 Peter 1:5-8)*.

Well, I trust you will think, and look upon, and experience these *Fruit* of Holy Spirit in a new way!

The Fruit of Holy Spirit is the incredible Life of Christ IN BELIEVERS manifested in so many different ways. What an incredible Life as a Christian to experience and enjoy!

Chapter 36

Holy Spirit of Power, of Love, and of Sound Mind

For God hath not given us the spirit of fear;
but of power, and of love, and of a sound mind.
2 Timothy 1:7

Nothing you have ever done, nothing you could ever do, will match the incomparable joy of letting Holy Spirit Live His Life through you.

All the gifts (fruit) of Holy Spirt come forth and abound when His LIFE is being experienced by you. These are Him manifesting Himself in our earthsuit, and include His Power, His Love, His Sound Mind as well as His Joy, His Peace, His Long-suffering, His Gentleness, His Goodness, His Faith, His Meekness, His Temperance…all the ones mentioned in 2 Timothy 1:7, Galatians 5:22-23 and elsewhere in the New Testament. In our text verse for this chapter Paul is telling Timothy about three aspects of Christ's Life that can counteract and negate any *spirit of fear* that combats His Presence.

Barbara and I visited a church one time back in the late 1970's. I remember telling the preacher that "all I want is peace in my life." We didn't find it there. But, when we went to Sagemont Church on May 18, 1980, and heard Pastor John Morgan preach on John chapter 3, "Ye Must Be Born Again," our lives began to change. We made an appointment to see him on Tuesday morning, May 20th. And in his office prayed to trust Jesus Christ as our Savior…God's Peace became ours.

There has been plenty of turmoil since that day, but the Peace of God and His Power, His Love, and His Sound Mind have been our portion through any turmoil we faced.

This verse is another that shows us that God has a Soul (Mind, Emotions and Will). His Soul includes His *Sound Mind*. It is the *Mind of Christ*. This verse is another that proves Christians have a *2nd soul* from our Spiritual birth, Christ's Soul as well as the old Adam-soul we were physically born with.

Think about it... *His Power* working in and through your life, actually His Life working in and through your earthsuit. Understanding and experiencing *His Love*...to you, and through you to others. Thinking and knowing and understanding with *His Mind*. Wow! No wonder Holy Spirit led Paul to tell Timothy, "God hath not given us the spirit of fear"! That is from the old Adam-life we were physically born with. That old Adam-life taught our old *natural* mind to *fear*. And when we live in that mind instead of *Christ's Mind*, *fear* can come and sometimes overtake us. Live in *Christ's Mind*. Live free from *fear*. Remember, Truth *makes* us free, and being *made* free IN Christ we are free indeed!

This is one verse that far too many Saints pass over without taking the time to really realize just what Christ IN us really brings to our earthsuit and our daily experiences. Just recognizing where *fear* comes from, and that it is not a part of who we are as Saints, can begin to give us thoughts that take us to Christ and all that He is IN us.

Do not let a lie keep you from Truth. Let Truth *make* you free and lead you to enjoy your birthright: *Holy Spirit's Power, His Love, His Sound Mind*.

Holy Spirit will bear fruit in our earthsuit that provides whatever resource we need for any situation.

Chapter 37

The Good Shepherd and His Sheep

I am the good shepherd:
the good shepherd giveth his life for the sheep.
John 10:11

In chapter 38 we will take a somewhat detailed look at the 23rd Psalm, where God tells us that He is our Shepherd. A beautiful Psalm. A beautiful description of so much that our Shepherd provides for us. But, let us look first at Jesus' detailing Himself as our Good Shepherd and some very interesting aspects of our relationship and fellowship with Him. (for a more complete look at our Good Shepherd and we as His sheep, see the last section, 13 chapters, of my book, *all i want is JESUS! – vol. 1, all i want is His Shepherding*)

The parable Jesus gives in John 10 details some great points about His Shepherding. See if you can picture how His description of the interaction of a shepherd with his flock of sheep in Israel relates to His interaction with you.

> Verily, verily, I say unto you, He that entereth not by the door into the sheepfold, but climbeth up some other way, the same is a thief and a robber. But he that entereth in by the door is the shepherd of the sheep. To him the porter openeth; and the sheep hear his voice: and he calleth his own sheep by name, and leadeth them out. And when he putteth forth his own sheep, he goeth before them, and the sheep follow him: for they know his voice. And a stranger will they not follow, but will flee from him: for they know not the voice of strangers. This parable spake Jesus unto them; but they understood not what things they were which he spake unto them. Then said Jesus unto them again, Verily, verily, I say unto

you, I am the door of the sheep. All that ever came before me are thieves and robbers: but the sheep did not hear them. I am the door: by me if any man enter in, he shall be saved, and shall go in and out, and find pasture. The thief cometh not, but for to steal, and to kill, and to destroy: I am come that they might have life, and that they might have it more abundantly. John 10:1-10

In verses 1-5 Jesus first gives us a good look at an earthly shepherd and his care for his sheep. The shepherd enters into the sheepfold where the sheep stay at night. He enters only by the door; there is only one door to the sheepfold. Thieves and robbers enter not at the door, but try to climb up another way. The porter (doorkeeper/watchman) knows the shepherd, and opens the door only for the shepherd and his sheep. Shepherds provided this protection in the dark hours of the night as part of their care for their sheep.

But Jesus tells us not only of the care and protection for the sheep at night, but of the interaction between the shepherd and his sheep during the day. Things like calling out to his sheep when he comes to get them in the morning to take them to the pasture he has picked out for them, for food and water. And Jesus tells of two of the most astounding facts that every shepherd and all his sheep have in common...the sheep *hear* and know *his voice*, and *he calls his sheep by name*, and then he leads them out to pasture. WOW! This is especially astounding since there can commonly be between 350-400 sheep that one earthly shepherd can manage in one flock. (Thank God, Christ has no limit for us as our Good Shepherd!)

Being as how most of us know nothing of real shepherds and sheep, we know nothing of these treasures except perhaps with some pet we have. But can you picture the second thing: the shepherd has a name for each sheep, and the sheep know their name. Jesus even goes so far as to tell us as *he goeth before them, the sheep follow him: for they know his voice*. What Jesus is telling us is of the *intimate knowledge* and *fellowship* of the shepherd with his sheep, and the deep interest the shepherd has with each one in his flock.

Now listen! The sheep will not follow a stranger, but will flee from him. They identify strangers from the sound of their voice. The Greek word translated *stranger* is *allotrios*, meaning *one whom they don't belong to, and don't trust.* Keep in mind sheep are virtually powerless and unable to defend themselves. Sheep are virtually mindless and unable to make good or wise decisions for themselves. Sheep are easily scared, easily distracted, easily misled, and easily harmed. Sheep need a shepherd they know and trust. This is the one thing God has given to sheep to protect them and nurture them.

Now in verse 7, Jesus begins to bring all this to a Spiritual context for us, His being OUR Good Shepherd. He equates with His being *the door of the sheep, the way IN*. He says everyone that has come before pretending or vehemently expressing they were the shepherd of God's people…they are thieves and robbers. And then Jesus declares *the sheep*, those who know God, *did not hear* (Greek: *akouo*, to hear with the ear of the mind) *them.*

And then Jesus gives two beautiful points before bringing us to verse 11. In verse 9, *I am the door; by Me if any man enter in, he shall be saved, and shall go in and out, and find pasture.* In verse 10, *I am come that they* (His sheep) *might have life (His Life), and that they might have it more abundantly* (His Life more abundantly). He is not talking about *things* or *trips* or *money*. He is talking about *Himself.* For more on this incredible Truth, see chapter 22.

So, verse 11, *I am the good shepherd: the good shepherd giveth his life for the sheep.* Don't miss this! Two ways Scripture speaks of Christ giving His life for us sheep. First, on His Cross, giving His Life in His death to pay the penalty for our sin and provide entrance to His sheepfold. Second, 24 hours a day…all the things mentioned so far. Protection, Provision, Guidance, Comfort, etc., etc. His Life is all that in us.

Thank God as a sheep of our Good Shepherd, we are "equipped" (with His Spirit and Soul) to be aware of strangers and "strange voices." Praise God we have our Lord Jesus Christ as our Good Shepherd, and His Life to be our Life.

Chapter 38

The Work of Our Good Shepherd

The LORD is my shepherd; I shall not want.
Psalm 23:1

In one brief statement, God sums up everything we need to know about Him being our Shepherd. "I shall not want." What *more* could any of God's sheep (child of God, Believer, Christian) *need* or *want*? That leads to one of my favorite sayings, "Christ is all I need, He is all I have, and He is all I want."

But in God's inestimable style He gives us the totality of His supply in measured, yet incalculable, words of wisdom. I have gone to great lengths to speak of these gifts in the last section of my book, *all i want is Jesus – vol. 1*. So, let me encourage you to read them in their entirety there, and see my brief highlights here. But, know this: your Good Shepherd will provide *all your want*, to where you *shall not want*.

He maketh me to lie down in green pastures
He leadeth me beside the still waters

The Hebrew *shavah*, is *to set, to place*. Our Good Shepherd picks out the best pastures for us, places where there is good feeding, good provision, plenty of grace (His activity). We need to keep in mind that our Shepherd takes it as His responsibility to provide *green pastures* for us and we get to *choose where* in *His pasture* we want to be. Interestingly these pastures are found in valleys, not mountaintops. There is plenty of *peace in the valley*. A *green pasture* is a place of provision.

Sheep must be led, not forced or driven. Still waters of rest and quietness provide security. Calm, cool, easy to drink from, satisfying any thirst. These first two provide PROVISION and PEACE...it is easy to lead sheep to a place of provision and peace.

He restoreth my soul
He leadeth me in the paths of righteousness for His name's sake

These two are PILLARS OF SUPPORT. *Restoreth my soul* is a Hebrew saying for *turn to Jehovah!* Holy Spirit knows we sheep are prone to wander away from our Shepherd. Abandonment to His Life will always take us on a *path of righteousness…for His name's sake.*

I will fear no evil for Thou art with me
Thy rod and Thy staff they comfort me

These two are the BEDROCK OF PATIENCE and CONTENTMENT. All sheep like comfort. With our Shepherd around (His presence) we can feel patience, contentment, and comfort. *Thou art with me* are four of the grandest words our Heart can know. Jesus is with us. There is nothing that confronts you and me that the Lord cannot handle. It is important to see, know, and experience the Shepherd's *rod* and *staff*. The *rod* for physical protection. The *staff* for mental management. The *rod* to ward off predators, and to get our attention if need be. The *staff* for guidance and clarity. Holy Spirit protects, teaches us, comforts us, and also guides us.

Thou preparest a table before me in the presence of mine enemies
Thou anointest my head with oil; my cup runneth over

These two speak of the DEMAND OF DEPENDENCY. Whether it is protection or provision, instruction, comfort, or guidance, we sheep must turn to our Shepherd and continuously depend on Him.

Goodness and mercy shall follow me all the days of my life
I will dwell in the house of the LORD forever

These two speak of DWELLING IN CHRIST. It really is important for Saints *today* to know that even though David wrote these words a little over 3,000 years ago, they are *huge for us!* The NT teaches that *we dwell in the house of the LORD now!* So think about that for a while.

And, it is Truth that God's *goodness* and *mercy* are with us all the days of our Life. His Life in us. Today. And forever. Hallelujah!

Our Good Shepherd tends to all our need, so that we shall not want.

Chapter 39

Truth (Christ) Makes Us Free

And ye shall know the truth, and the truth shall make you free...
If the Son therefore shall make you free, ye shall be free indeed.
John 8:32, 36

To this point in this book, God has given us a lot of His Truth. Him personified. One thing we must always stay cognizant of: Christ IS Truth. All Truth *makes us free.* Let us think more sincerely on this dramatic impact for our lives.

Since Christ IS Truth, the two are inseparable. That's why I put the two in the title of this chapter. Actually, verse 31, "Then said Jesus to those Jews which believed on Him, If ye continue in My word (*logos*, a Greek word meaning a word as the expression of intelligence), then are ye My disciples indeed," sets the stage for the profound statements in verses 32 and 36. Christ MAKES us free is a crucial Truth. It is a tragic falsehood that some translations misrepresent this as "Christ sets us free." There is a huge difference in *makes* and *sets*.

Now keep in mind, ever since the Garden of Eden our enemy has been after one thing with all his might: "yea, hath God said?" Diversion, dilution, deletion, disdain, distrust, distraction...any way he can get God's children to doubt or deviate from the Word(s) of God. This is the effort of some to use subtlety to get Christians to deviate and to use faulty or false translations. I don't blame them as such, just their not possessing the *Mind of Christ* to know Truth, or their using the *old mind* and missing Truth. Without going into that battle once more, let me give you a simple illustration to show the falsehood of *set free* in those verses.

Let's say someone has committed the crime. And they are arrested. A jury finds them guilty of some crime. A sentence of some kind is pronounced. Bondage in some form is the payment for the crime. They are not free any more. Now, for a good picture, think back to the old western movies when an outlaw's compadres would tear out the window of the back of the jail, blow a hole in the back wall, or simply come into the front of the jail with guns drawn and **set** the jailed outlaw *free*. Was the outlaw *completely* and *permanently free*, or just removed, most often temporarily, from the jail? But, IF a judge, or jury, or the Governor, reversed the verdict or pardoned the outlaw, the outlaw was **made** *free*, no longer with any guilt or bondage hanging over his head. *Made free* instead of *set free*. See the huge difference?

As a pastor for many years I spoke with numerous Saints who thought they had been *set free* but were still in bondage. Through Scriptural discipleship many were *made free* by Christ. No more bondage. Free.

Galatians 5:1, "Stand fast therefore in the liberty wherewith Christ hath **made** us *free*, and be not entangled again with the yoke of bondage." (Again, bad translations use *set*). Being **made** *free* speaks of the absolute, complete, permanent freedom we have as the result of the Redemption of Christ. Totally **MADE FREE** from the BONDAGE of the *old man*. Therefore, God says do not enter back into anything to do with the *old man*, the yoke of bondage.

Jesus has **MADE** Saints **FREE** from ANY GUILT. In fact, God has said, "There is therefore now no condemnation to them which are in Christ..." Romans 8:1. Would you rather be **set** *free*, basically temporarily, OR **made** *free* permanently?

The modern translations, and the counterfeit idea of *set*, are an example of one of many very subtle tools our enemy uses to move Believers away from *what God hath said*. Those WALKING IN THE SPIRIT and TESTING THE SPIRITS will know the difference by the *grace* of God, in due time, with good fellowship with Holy Spirit.

Don't you really want to know if you absolutely have THE Word of God in your hands? Also, anytime you see *Truth* in Scripture, you can substitute *Jesus* and still be handling Truth. Verses 32 and 36 make that explicitly clear.

Made free by Christ is the only Truthful freedom.

Chapter 40

The Peace of Christ

*Peace I leave with you, My peace I give unto you:
not as the world giveth, give I unto you.
Let not your heart be troubled,
neither let it be afraid.*
John 14:27

Nothing transcends any trouble, fear, worry, anxiety, doubt, guilt, or condemnation like the Peace of Christ. So, we must find out the Who, when, where, what, and how of Living in His Peace. In this chapter we will talk about the *Who,* the *when,* and the *where* His Peace becomes our peace. In chapter 41 we will talk about the *what* and the *how*.

The *Who* is Jesus Christ. Jesus tells us His Peace is different from anything the world can give us. It is different in a way that is Truthful peace, the peace that passes understanding by those who are not Saints. We who are Saints can understand His Peace.

What we need to know, realize, and not ever forget IS that when we experience Christ's Peace we are (or, have been) experiencing Him. Yes. Experiencing Him. Not just some nebulous peace that is better than anything we have ever experienced, but real contact and a real experiencing of Christ in and through us. Wow! How wonderful is that? How marvelous is that? How REAL is that?

Far too many Saints do not think it possible to *experience Christ.* Too many pray to the *Great Man in the Sky.* Too many try to get their prayers to break through some mystical ceiling to reach God. He is IN us. We experience Him day in and day out, and far too many do not realize it.

Ok. The *when.* Jesus tells us anytime our heart may be troubled, or afraid, that is *when* we need to experience His Peace. *When* it MIGHT be troubled/afraid. Actually, at ALL times *ahead* of any *troubling* or *fear.* Not just when it IS troubled/afraid. Jesus said, *Let not your Heart BE troubled, or afraid*. Do not let it BE troubled, or afraid. Anytime. And actually, this is a parabolic teaching. IF we are Living in the Heart of Christ, we will never experience any *troubling* or *fear*. Those two never enter the Heart of Christ, which is ours by birthright (New Birth). All the other feelings or thoughts mentioned in the first sentence of the first paragraph come only in the *natural heart*. Remember this!

It is amazing how many Saints say they trust the Lord for everything. They say they believe God is in control. They say nothing can cause them to cease resting in Christ. And then something happens that brings trouble to their heart. Wrong heart. Oh, wow. Do you see the transition from *not letting the Heart be troubled* or *afraid ANYTIME*…to all of a sudden there is trouble/fear in the heart (old heart)? Christ's Peace is present in our *Supernatural Heart* ALL the time. It is Him. It is His Heart. He is that Peace. Nothing should keep us from having His Peace at any time.

So, the *where*. Right here is a big answer to our enjoying the Peace of Christ always, all the time. It is in the *where*. This is what I have mentioned in the two previous paragraphs. The *where* is wrapped up in the Trichotomy of a Believer (see diagram and writing that follows in chapter 8). The *Supernatural Heart* of Christ's Soul is in a Saint…in every Saint. His *Heart*. That is the *where*. His *Heart* will always be Peaceful in us ALL the time.

Now listen. There can be NO trouble or fear in *Christ's Heart*. Do you think for a second that Christ was ever *troubled in His Heart? Afraid?* No. Never. Do we have *Christ's Heart?* Yes. It is a part of the completeness we have IN Christ. So, be sure to know this: *when* any trouble/fear comes that might *trouble our heart/cause fear*, be sure to know (and not forget!), it can only come IF we are living out of the *natural heart* still residing in us. THAT *where* can, and often does, yield a *troubled/fearful heart*. But God has given us the choice, and His Power to choose, *His Heart* over the *natural heart* in any and all situations. Therefore, we can live in *His Peace* that He has given us (His Presence and Person, our Life, IN us) IF we choose to abandon to His Life as *our* Life, His All as *our* All. Well, amen.

That still leaves the *what* and the *how*, two very important ingredients to Living in the Peace of Christ. The *what* is beautiful to know and understand. We who have experienced His Peace know what His Peace is, and what it is like. It is like nothing the world has to offer. But, the *how* is most important to know and understand to experience Christ's Peace continuously, all the time. Too much teaching tells us *all* except the *how*. Or, too often we get a wrong *how*, or incomplete/inadequate *how* which leaves us just as weak and incompetent to deal with the *troubled/fearful heart* as if we didn't have any teaching at all. You may be amazed at *how* (no pun intended) easy, uncomplicated, and predictably God-inspired is the Truth of the *how*. Don't miss these two in chapter 41!

When peace like a river, attendeth my way…Thou hast taught me to say, it is well, it is well with my Soul…actually, His Soul I Live in (that is why I capitalized Soul at the end). There is no peace in the old soul.

Chapter 41

What Is It To Have Christ's Peace? And How?

*Thou wilt keep him in perfect peace, whose mind
is stayed on thee: because he trusteth in thee.
Isaiah 26:3*

In chapter 40, we found the *Peace of Christ* that Christians possess, John 14:27, a gift of Christ to all His Saints. Yet, we also mentioned that too many do not experience that possession as much as they should. That is very sad. It is like having 10 million dollars in the bank with an income of 10,000 dollars each month to add to the 10 million, and then living as if we have zero dollars in the bank and only 1 thousand dollars a month income. Talk about a *fretting* and *fearful heart!* I suppose it isn't a stretch to add it might be a *confused* heart, a *conflicted* heart, a *crushed* heart.

But we found the *Who,* the *when,* and the *where* His Peace becomes our peace. Wonderful Truths. Yet, all that is just a part of the Truth as a whole. And the whole is needed to truthfully *experience* the Peace of Christ. So, let us finish what we started last chapter, and get us complete in Truth relating to the Peace of Christ, discovering the *what* and the *how* of Living in the Peace of Christ all the time.

The *what.* I have loved Isaiah 26:3 for many, many years. Just stop and meditate on Isaiah's words given him by Holy Spirit for our good. *Thou* (God Almighty). *Wilt keep him* (that's you and me as His kids). *In perfect peace* (*perfect*, not anything less! *peace*, really our heart's desire). *Whose mind* (now, don't forget, we have seen *which* mind that is for us!). *Is stayed on Thee* (oh, oh, oh...we're getting close to completeness of this Truth!). *Because he trusteth in Thee* (Hallelujah!). Hang on, now. These last two qualities are going to grip you completely...

The Peace God as described for us here and in John 14 is a marvelous *what.* I don't know about you, but I guess out of all things God could give me, His Peace is about as huge as anything. Yes, salvation is the most important, but that is ours when we are Born Again and have become His New Creation. Done. Settled. A Saint. A Child of God. Sins forgiven. *Ticket* to heaven punched. Yet, with all we face day in and day out, the *Peace of God* is one gift that supersedes in importance and in totality most all other gifts God could give us.

I remember going to church a few years before being Born Again. I was looking for *peace*. I had no peace in my life at the time. And I told the preacher that was what I wanted most. But I never found it there in almost two years. And we quit going.

The *Peace of Christ* cannot easily be put into words. That is because of the *Who* and the *what*. It is simply experiencing Jesus Christ and not some feeling. I picture it somewhat like this: I am walking along life's path and suddenly I feel a touch – perhaps a grabbing of my hand, perhaps an arm around my shoulders – and I look up and *see* (with the *Spiritual* eyes God has given me, and every Believer) the Lord Jesus Christ right next to me, and it is Him touching me. Have you ever experienced Him like that? You might have and didn't know or recognize it was Him. A calm, a comfort, a confidence, or a complete warmth engulfed your Soul. You just knew everything was OK. All was well with your Soul at that moment. THAT is *what* the *Supernatural Peace of Christ* is.

Ok. *Perfect peace* is a *Supernatural Peace*. A *Spiritual Peace*. Not of the world, not as the world giveth. Only God can give His *Supernatural, Spiritual Peace*. Amen. And He says He wants to, and will, to *keep us* in His perfect, *Supernatural, Spiritual Peace* based on two things we *do*. Yes, we are always looking for something we can *do* to get something from God. Well, here are two things…

First, we must STAY in the *Mind of Christ*. God has given us His Mind. God has given us the capacity to *choose* which mind we live in. We must *choose* to *stay* in His Mind. God has clearly told us through the prophet Isaiah. Why is this so difficult for many Saints? The *old mind* is a mind of turmoil, trouble, trepidation, and other terrible thoughts that steal the *Peace of Christ* from any Saints traversing in the wrong mind.

Secondly, we must TRUST in the Provider and Keeper of the *Peace of Christ*. Almighty God, Creator of Heaven, earth, and mankind is the One who has promised to provide and keep in *Perfect Peace* His children whose Mind is stayed on Him. For some Godly assistance in keeping your Mind on Him…

> Finally, brethren, whatsoever things are true, whatsoever things are honest, whatsoever things are just, whatsoever things are pure, whatsoever things are lovely, whatsoever things are of good report; if there be any virtue, and if there be any praise, think on these things. Philippians 4:8

These are the things Holy Spirit through the apostle Paul gave us to *think* about, to keep our Mind on, for the *Peace of God* and the *God of Peace* to show Himself with us. Thinking of other things can steal away the *Peace of God* and the *God of Peace*.

There isn't a Saint alive that does not hunger for the *Peace of Christ, His Peace* that Unbelievers cannot see, grasp, comprehend, or understand.

Oh, the joy of residing in the Presence of Christ, and He Himself enveloping us in His Peace of Himself. Keeping our Mind stayed on Him, trusting completely in Him. Do you feel His touch this moment?

Chapter 42

Learning To BE Content

*Not that I speak in respect of want: for I have learned,
in whatsoever state I am, therewith to be content.*
Philippians 4:11

The Greek for *content* in our text is *autarkes*. It actually comes partially from *arkeo*, which is the word translated *content* in 1 Timothy 6:6-8 and Hebrews 13:5. (See end of chapter for these and more verses). *Autarkes* describes being self-sufficient in a good sense, or adequate, or being satisfied with what one has. *Arkeo* means being sufficient or satisfying. God used that to describe His Grace being sufficient in 2 Corinthians 12:9 (for Paul, and us).

God gives *contentment*. The world breeds *discontent* (1 John – 3 things).
> Love not the world, neither the things that are in the world. If any man love the world, the love of the Father is not in him. For all that is in the world, the lust of the flesh, and the lust of the eyes, and the pride of life, is not of the Father, but is of the world. 1 John 2:15-16

How could anyone be *content* if the Love of the Father is not present? Clearly, this is a statement that shows us someone who is living in the *old, natural* soul, loving the *flesh* and things of the world.

ALL advertising is for that purpose. *Discontentment* breeds purchasing. The most ridiculous *ad* – to a sound mind - is the roadside sign with NO *product* advertised that says, "Does advertising work? Just did!" The advertising company is saying that when your eyes glancing around see their board, their sign has *worked*. HOW did that *advertising* work? No *product* was advertised. However, what is in their minds is that you will *buy* their *advertisement* for you to *advertise* on their sign. And their sign is to tell everyone that just *seeing* a product is enough to become *discontent* if you don't have it, and you will then *want* it.

That is counterfeit to Truth. Truth tells us God has taken it upon Himself to provide so that we won't *want* (Psalm 23, chapter 38) and provide all our *need* (Philippians 4:19, chapter 45). Truth tells us a *want* is not a *need*. Paul was emphasizing that! Advertisers are trying to convince the looker that just seeing the sign *works*. Sadly, for too many, it must, or the sign owners would put something else up there to try and get businesses to advertise there. The billboard sign people are trying to convince companies that IF they had their message on the sign, people would buy the advertised product. Much of advertising is an effort to drive an illegitimate *want* in the consumer to the point of becoming *discontent* with what God has provided.

From a financial standpoint, what is one of the best practical ways to *learn* contentment, or *force yourself* to be content? "Every dollar has a NAME on it BEFORE the month begins." This is deciding before every month begins just how you will spend your income. The *names* come from having a Monthly Spending Plan. This practice aids in growing into being *content* with God's provision…and living on it.

Look again in Philippians, ch.4, at what God has told us in v.11. *I have learned, in whatsoever state I am, therewith to be content.* Two facts jump right out at us. One, *I have learned.* Learned. Contentment can be *learned.* And should be. In fact, IF we have NOT *learned* to be *content,* that is where we start. Secondly, *in whatsoever state I am in, therewith to be content.* This is not Texas, Oklahoma, New Mexico, Louisiana, or Arkansas. It is *whatsoever circumstance* I am in. No matter what our circumstance, our condition, our job, our bank account, etc. We are to learn to BE *content* with whatever God gives us, where He places us, whatever He is doing in our lives. With *contentment* comes *peace*. With God, we will have both.

With verses 12 & 13, God speaks through Paul about Living in Christ, not depending on the world.

> I know both how to be abased, and I know how to abound: every where and in all things I am instructed both to be full and to be hungry, both to abound and to suffer need. I can do all things through Christ which strengtheneth me.

What a beautiful, peaceful Life. Christ's Life. Full or hungry. Abounding or suffering need. Peace. Joy. Contentment.

It is imperative that we look back also at Philippians 4:6-9 and know that if we are Living in the *Mind of Christ*, we will be thinking ON the correct things, which breed *contentment,* then the God of Peace and the Peace of God will be ours.

> But godliness with contentment is great gain. For we brought nothing into this world, and it is certain we can carry nothing out. And having food and raiment let us be therewith content. 1 Timothy 6:6-8
>
> Let your conversation be without covetousness; and be content with such things as ye have: for he hath said, I will never leave thee, nor forsake thee. Hebrews 13:5
>
> Be careful for nothing; but in every thing by prayer and supplication with thanksgiving let your requests be made known unto God. And the peace of God, which passeth all understanding, shall keep your hearts and minds through Christ Jesus. Finally, brethren, whatsoever things are true, whatsoever things are honest, whatsoever things are just, whatsoever things are pure, whatsoever things are lovely, whatsoever things are of good report; if there be any virtue, and if there be any praise, think on these things. Those things, which ye have both learned, and received, and heard, and seen in me, do: and the God of peace shall be with you. Philippians 4:6-9

Now listen, a mind stayed on *peace* and *contentment* cannot ever get *depressed.* The *Mind of Christ* is the only Mind that can guarantee this. We will look in some detail about Christians and *depression* in chapter 44, but just know that as long as we are abiding in the *Mind of Christ* there can be *no depression* in us.

The LORD is my Shepherd. I shall not want. That is contentment personified.

Chapter 43

Never Be Offended

*Great peace have they which love thy law:
and nothing shall offend them.*
Psalm 119:165

Right up front I spot this second mentioning of *great peace* (like we saw in Isaiah 26:3, chapter 41). Wow! Beautiful! Incredible! I know of little in this world that can equal day-in and day-out enjoying the Peace of God. And here God tells us two things:

1. *Great peace* have they which love His law. That's a shocker, isn't it? We New Testament Believers are all big into *we are not under law, but under grace*. Yes. But, God's law has not been done away with. Jesus told us He came to fulfill the law. He never says He did away with what is the law, what is in the law, what is good in the law. He fulfilled the law. AND, He fulfills the law every day in millions of Christians all around the world. He, Who is our Life, when He is unhindered from filling us completely fulfills the law in our earthsuit. Amen! His fulfilling the law brings *great peace* to us in and out. Inwardly in our soul. Outwardly through our earthsuit. Inwardly to us. Outwardly to others.

What does it mean to you to be aware that the law has not been done away with? The 10 Commandments have not been dismissed, but are to be fulfilled by Christ through us? God's law is still what He desires to *Live through us*, just not *by us*.
This eliminates a lot of confusion for many Christians.

This takes all the pressure off *us*, and puts it on Christ. And He is the only One who has ever *kept* the law in its entirety. And He has no difficulty doing so *through us* when we are abandoned to Him and not quenching Holy Spirit. Well, amen! That brings joy to my Heart of His in me (don't forget the trichotomy!).

2. And then, just think of how that affects our interaction with others. God tells us, *and nothing shall offend them* (those who have the *great peace* that comes with *loving God's law*). THINK OF THAT! Nothing. Not one thing that comes our way. If we can *never be* offended, then not one thing *someone else* can do, or does do to us affects or hinders our interaction with someone. Nothing. *Nothing shall offend them (us/you and me).* Hallelujah!

Of course every time I hear or say this, it makes me think of my friend, Michael Wells. He always said, "Psalm 119:165 in effect says, *If you can be offended, you deserve to be offended.*" What he said was if we love the law of God, not only will *great peace* be enjoyed by us, but nothing will offend us...AND if we are offended, there is something wrong in our *abiding/Living* in Christ. Therefore we *deserve* to be offended. Wow! That should get our attention.

We can know that there is something God has said, something God has directed, something God has intended for us that is *not right with us* IF we are getting offended in any way by any one. Jesus never got offended. Jesus IN us can never get offended. *Flesh* can easily get offended. Offended? That comes from living in the *flesh*, and not in the Spirit. Galatians chapter 5. It is as easy as that.

I choose to keep in the Mind of Christ, loving God's law, and embracing God's peace, and to never be offended.

Chapter 44

NO Depression EVER

*Heaviness in the heart of man maketh it stoop:
but a good word maketh it glad.*
Proverbs 12:25

The Hebrew word translated *heaviness* could have just as easily been translated *fear, dread, anxious, sorrow, troubled, afraid, or deep anxiety*. Wow! That is quite a list of *feelings* that are all too common for a lot of people, including Christians. Now, we saw in Chapter 42 how discontentment breeds wrong thinking and wrong activity. Philippians 4:4, 6-9 really tell us what to expect if we Live in the Mind of Christ, avoiding the wrong thoughts that bring on the feelings God mentions here in Proverbs 12:25.

Then look at the result of these wrong feelings: a *stooped heart*. The Hebrew word translated *stoop* is a word that literally means *to depress, to bow down*. It was used as a show of recognizing something as superior, even a person. Now think about this for a moment. The feelings mentioned in the first paragraph are such that can make someone's heart *stoop, bow down to something superior, be depressed*. Hence, this is how someone's feelings lead to what is known as *depression*.

Now, let me make it clear. *Depression* can only come to the *natural mind/heart*. But, remember every Christian has *that mind/heart* still in us, as well as the Mind/Heart of Christ. WHEN a Believer functions in the *old mind/heart* their thinking and feeling can lead to being *depressed*. HOWEVER, that should never be the case with a Believer. We are to Live ONLY in the Mind/Heart of Christ within.

Apart from that position of Living, we must not miss that God tells us it is a *good word* that makes the heart glad. What is that *good word* for us. HIS WORD. So, let us investigate this verse more thoroughly.

God's Words Bring *Life*

We will list some words that describe feelings possible to have, and give God's Good Word that counteract these, and give us His thoughts from *His Mind* that we should be Living with.

fear – Isaiah 26:3, *Thou wilt keep him in perfect peace, whose mind is stayed on Thee: because he trusteth in Thee*; 1 Peter 5:7, *Cast all your care upon Him; for He careth for you*; and 2 Timothy 1:7 (refer back to chapter 36).

worry – Philippians 4:4, 6-9, *Rejoice in the Lord always: and again I say, rejoice…Be careful for nothing; but in every thing by prayer and supplication with thanksgiving let your requests be made known unto God. And the peace of God, which passeth all understanding, shall keep your hearts and minds through Christ Jesus. Finally, brethren, whatsoever things are true, whatsoever things are honest, whatsoever things are just, whatsoever things are pure, whatsoever things are lovely, whatsoever things are of good report; if there be any virtue, and if there be any praise, think on these things. Those things, which ye have both learned, and received, and heard, and seen in me, do: and the God of peace shall be with you.*

doubt – Romans 8:28, *And we know that all things work together for good to them that love God, to them who are the called according to His purpose*; Philippians 4:19, *But my God shall supply all your need according to His riches in glory by Christ Jesus*; John 10:22-27, *And it was at Jerusalem the feast of the dedication, and it was winter. And Jesus walked in the temple in Solomon's porch. Then came the Jews round about Him, and said unto Him, How long dost Thou make us to doubt? If Thou be the Christ, tell us plainly. Jesus answered them, I told you, and ye believed not: the works that I do in my Father's name, they bear witness of Me. But ye believe not, because ye are not of my sheep, as I said unto you. My sheep hear My voice, and I know them, and they follow Me.* James 1:5-8, *If any of you lack wisdom, let him ask of God, that giveth to all men liberally, and upbraideth not; and it shall be given him. But let him ask in faith, nothing wavering. For he that wavereth is like a wave of the sea driven with the wind and tossed. For let not that man think that he shall receive any thing of the Lord. A double-minded man is unstable in all his ways.*

guilt/condemnation – Romans 8:1, *There is therefore now no condemnation to them which are in Christ Jesus, who walk not after the flesh, but after the Spirit.* 1 John 1:9, *If we confess our sins, He is faithful and just to forgive us our sins, and to cleanse us from all unrighteousness.*

God's Words Bring *Life*

Now, listen. The overriding Truth for Christians suffering from heaviness, a troubled heart, fear, anxiety, and ultimately *depression*, is that they are functioning out of the wrong soul, the wrong mind, the wrong emotions, the wrong will, the wrong heart. Christ's Mind/Soul/Heart does not think what these erroneous Christians are thinking. Christ's Mind/Soul/Heart does not go there. We must wake up and realize *depression* does not *suit* a Believer. This is a statement of *look* or *fit*. *Depression* certainly doesn't *look* good on a Believer. And it does not *fit* us. *Depression* is not acceptable, appropriate, or in accord with who we are as Christians. AND, none of the thoughts that lead to *depression* are acceptable, appropriate, or in accord with who we are as Christians.

Abide in the *Mind of Christ* and you will eliminate any & ALL *depression* from your life. *Depression* is not His Life.

God's Good Words bring gladness (in His Heart) and keep away thoughts leading to anything not of God.

Chapter 45

Our Divine Supply

> But my God shall supply all your need
> according to His riches in glory by Christ Jesus.
> Philippians 4:19

Trust God for His supply, then live on it. That has been Barbara's and my conviction for financial decisions ever since we were introduced to Truth like Philippians 4:19. We have lived debt-free and trusting in/waiting on God's supply since 1981.

The Apostle Paul was telling the Philippians that HIS God, Who is OUR God and was theirs, WILL SUPPLY ALL OUR NEED. That alone is a dynamic big enough to settle a whole lot of issues for Saints. When it gets down to the so-called *bottom line*, there is little that can bring peace and joy more than knowing that our *need* WILL be supplied. But, it is imperative that we ACKNOWLEDGE and KNOW that OUR GOD is the One Who will do this. Christianity has seemingly forgotten (or in these days has seldom been taught) that life is all about OUR GOD, NOT US; His Life, His ways & not ours (or, the enemy's!).

Think about it. We have GOD Who has told us that it is His determination to supply all we will ever need. Wow! What, in this life, do we have to be anxious about? What do we have to worry about? What do we have to be distraught about? Our GOD is going to supply all we ever need. He has taken it upon Himself to be responsible for our supply.

And lest we get in a tizzy thinking as to HOW in this world can He provide for ALL His children…provide ALL our need…God tells us further that He will provide this *according to His riches in glory by Christ Jesus.* Few ever think about, mention, dwell, or emphasize this critical caveat (one definition of *caveat* is *words given to prevent misunderstanding*). Well, lest we misunderstand, God says "MY supply is unlimited…according to

MY riches in glory by Christ Jesus." Never forget: there is nothing the *presence of Christ* cannot provide. And every Believer possesses Christ within...*His presence*. That brings with it *His provision*.

Now listen. God's provision for ALL our need includes not just financial needs. It includes ANY need, ANY time. Throughout Scripture God has shown Himself faithful to bring His Supply to His people at any moment they had a need. The same is for us today.

So, here are three things I can think of that would prevent, hinder, or detour God's supply to His saints...and yet, there is never any lack of His supply available...

1. unbelief. An *Unbelieving* Saint is one who has been Born Again, *but* (this is what I call an Unholy But) does not believe God for all that God has revealed to His Saints about life here and now. They believe He will take us to heaven one day, but *supply any and all our need right now*, that's a little too far-fetched for some Believers. This *unbelief* leads to taking unbiblical actions to procure needs, and usually *wants*. And God has told us He cannot/will not work in one's life who is living in unbelief.

2. waste. Many Believers have no sense of stewardship. I think this is because of little, if any, teaching of good, practical, Scriptural lifestyles and management. If everyone 50 years or older would take just a few minutes to think back over their life, they would stagger at the memories of the huge waste of money for frivolous things that were nothing but a momentary happiness that faded with the next sunrise. How can one dollar spent today that is meaningless for the future compare to having nothing in our pockets at some date in the future when there is a *need*? And, if everyone 10-20 years of age were made to sit down, listen to, and get into a discussion of the numerous issues facing them for the next 70 years or so...how many could see the necessity of financial stewardship their entire life. Having fun, getting something to make you happy for the moment, and going & doing for some sort of *high* CANNOT take the place of responsible stewardship for the need now and a need in the future. I have been telling folks for a long time: "You have been smoking, drinking, eating, and travelling away your comfortable retirement. How does that work for you now that you are 65 and broke?" And they want me to have empathy for them? Or, to help them out from the *hard-earned, did-without, sensible and God-directed practical* *stewardship dollars* in my possession? I may have been born at night; it just wasn't last night!

Need more advice from God? Try these admonitions:
> No man can serve two masters: for either he will hate the one, and love the other; or else he will hold to the one, and despise the other. Ye cannot serve God and mammon. Therefore, I say unto you, Take no thought for your life, what ye shall eat, or what ye shall drink; nor yet for your body, what ye shall put on. Is not the life more than meat, and the body than raiment? Matthew 6:24-25

And then, after giving illustrations of how God supplies the need of fowls of the air, lilies of the field, the grass of the field, and asking *shall He not much more clothe you, O ye of little faith?* (v.30), Holy Spirit led Matthew to conclude with:
> Therefore take no thought, saying, What shall we eat? or, What shall we drink? or, Wherewithal shall we be clothed? For after all these things do the Gentiles seek: for your heavenly Father knoweth that you have need of all these things. But seek ye first the kingdom of God, and His righteousness; and all these things will be added unto you. Take therefore no thought for the morrow: for the morrow shall take thought for the things of itself. Sufficient unto the day is the evil thereof. Matthew 6:31-34

Wow! Take no thought (question) for all your need…but, *seek ye first the kingdom of God, and His righteousness; AND ALL THESE THINGS WILL BE ADDED UNTO YOU.* That leads us to the third thing I spoke of earlier:

3. lack of worship in Truth. Worship is *showing worth, 'worth-ship'*. If Saints were truthfully worshipping (showing worth) God, they would *hang* on every word from God. The Holy Scriptures would have a more significant place and impact in EVERY Saint's life. And intense study of significant verses, including seeking out the Greek behind the translation could lead to more BELIEVING by more Saints. The Truths of verses like the ones I have mentioned already in this chapter (as well as the multitude in the rest of this book) are sufficient to change many Saints' minds on how they will make decisions regarding the procurement of their needs. The lack of Truthful worship of God today is staggering.

Now listen to a poignant statement from the man Barbara and I first learned God's Truths on financial matters:

John Morgan (Pastor, Sagemont Church, Houston, Texas): "Man chooses the supplier of his need. God or satan. Truth or deception. Obedience or disobedience. Freedom or bondage. (satan's deception & disobedience always lead to bondage)." Wow! I remember first hearing those words, and can also remember the impact they made on decisions we made to make changes from doing things the world's way (devil's influence) to God's way.

And one more for now…

John Morgan, "The devil will always say, 'If your God won't give it to you now, just sign here. I will.'" It is my hope and prayer that everyone reading these words will CHOOSE to do things God's Way in all financial matters! This chapter is straight to the point of whether we will Live *Trusting God for His supply, and Living on it,* or not.

And, most people today are basically living a lie. They trust the devil's supply: credit, false/fake money.

I like Dave Ramsey's comment: "Live like no one else today, so that you can live like no one else later on."

I remember my grandparents and parents talking about the days when the only way to purchase something was to pay with cash. There was no personal credit with almost every business. They made comments about those days such as: "You did whatever you had to do, to do whatever you wanted to do." "You made do."

One of the oldest gentlemen I saw come to Christ for salvation was Neil Oldham. Way up in his 70's, Neil got Born Again during a crusade we had in our church with evangelist Herman Cramer preaching. Neil and I were sitting on his back porch one day in 1989 (I was visiting with Neil as he cracked pecans from some of the big pecan trees in his yard with his homemade cracker). We were talking about finances and Neil stopped what he was doing. He looked straight at me, a little more than half his age at the time. He said, "Preacher. There was a day back when I was growing up where if God had not provided the cash for something, we didn't buy it." That was a time long before credit, the devil's false provision, was available.

Think on that.

Trust God for His supply, and live on it. That is The Math of Life. Christ's Life. For any and all our need.

Chapter 46

From Faith to Faith

Thou therefore, my son, be strong in the grace that is in Christ Jesus.
And the things that thou hast heard of me among many witnesses,
the same commit thou to faithful men,
who shall be able to teach others also.
2 Timothy 2:1-2

Certainly one of the first times I remember these two verses being brought to my attention, or perhaps really noticing and grasping the thoughts therein, was in my first class when I started seminary (1st semester at Southwestern Seminary, Fall, 1981, Dr. Roy Fish, Professor). It was the focal verse of the Personal Evangelism class I had signed up for. Dr. Fish pointed out *4 generations* of Saints (Paul, Timothy, faithful ones, and then others) of which *the things that thou has heard of me* were passed from one to another.

Romans 1:17 speaks what Habakkuk 2:4 talks of, *and the just shall live by His faith*. The *Faith* of Scripture is the *Faith of God/Christ*. Christ's Faith breeds faithfulness (faithful ones who teach/share with other faithful ones). *Faithful ones* LIVE *strong in the grace* that is IN (of) Christ Jesus (v.1) – see also ch.48. This Life of Grace (His Life, His Grace, His Power, His Working) is how Christianity is passed from one *generation* to another (one Saint to another).

It is Christ's Faith, not ours originally. It is His Faith that becomes *ours* when we *believe/trust* Him and He solidifies our believing/trusting. When we are *abandoned to Him*, that brings about His Grace.

His Grace is His keeping ALL of the 2nd Covenant (Testament). God gave the people of Israel the 1st Covenant, and the agreement between them was that they would all keep ALL of the Laws. They didn't do a good job of that, did they? When God gave the 2nd Covenant, He said "I see yall didn't do so well with the 1st, I don't expect you would do any better with the 2nd, so I am sending Myself (in an earthsuit as Jesus Christ) to fully keep the 2nd, AND...I will put Myself IN EACH SAINT and will keep the Laws fully in each one." Our agreement (in essence, our part) in the New Life of the New Testament is four things: believe, trust, receive, enjoy.

Believe/trust (Exchanged Life), receive (Abiding Life), enjoy (Grace Life). That is some great news of the 2nd Covenant. When we are Born Again, God exchanges our *old life* (lost, human spirit with a little *s* - old nature, sin nature) for *Christ's New Life* IN US (Holy Spirit, His Nature, sinless Nature). In everything in life, our *job* is to believe, trust, receive, and enjoy...all from His Life in us. His Grace (His doing the work or keeping) is His job.

His Life IN US keeps ALL of the laws when we are abandoned to Him. His Life IN US does all the *doing* of Christianity. We contribute nothing. We bring nothing to the table. We have nothing to contribute.

Now listen! This is so important and we must never forget this, or take any credit for any of it: the only ultimate Source of Divine activity in all Spiritual Life is God Himself. That is Colossians 1:27, Christ in us, our hope. None of *us*. In our flesh dwelleth no good thing, especially any Divine activity.

Therefore, when Scripture speaks of *being strong in the grace that is in Christ Jesus*, it is talking about our being abandoned to Him so that He can show forth His Life, His Power, His Working...that is His Grace (more in ch.48).

AND...that is how *all these things* are passed from *each who is abandoned to God, to another who is abandoned to God.*

Truthfully, being faithful is to be continuously abandoned. Thereby enjoying the Grace that is in Christ Jesus.

Chapter 47

Faithful In The Least

He that is faithful in that which is least is faithful also in much:
and he that is unjust in the least is unjust also in much.
Luke 16:10

I love this verse! It is a simple principle of Life. God tells us in the most uncomplicated terms: if we are *faithful* (Greek: *pistos,* trustworthy/fidelity) in the *least* (little things), we WILL be *faithful, pistos,* in *much* (big things or many things). It is in a context of stewardship, not of being possessors...of having to give an account of our handling of something belonging to someone else. But, then, God says that if we have been unjust (Greek: *adikos,* undependable/fails expectations) in the *least*, we WILL be *unjust, adikos,* in the greater or many things.

If a person has been trustworthy with relatively unimportant things, *he will* (and therefore can be trusted) *be trustworthy* with relatively important things, or *much more* important things. On the other hand, if a person has been untrustworthy with relatively unimportant things, *he will* (and therefore cannot be trusted) *be untrustworthy/a cheat/a defrauder* in greater, many, much more important things.

How more clearly could our Lord express this? How more simple to read or hear and understand could His Words be? So, what is left is to explore the application of His Words to life itself.

First, it is easy to see that an unbeliever/infidel really is most likely to be *unjust* with things. That is the nature of an unbeliever/infidel. But, we as Saints choose whether to live in *old self* which is just as *unjust* naturally as with an unbeliever/infidel, OR we as Saints choose to *abandon* to Christ for *His Life* to Live through our earthsuit as a *faithful* steward.

Think about the Life of Christ. He is the only One who has EVER been *faithful* in ALL things. Christ IN us will be *faithful* in ALL things as we are abandoned to Him.

For us, the easiest thing is to *recognize* and *realize* that when we are abandoned to Christ, He will be *faithful* in that which is *least*, the *little* things. We know what the *little* things are...the things no one really wants to do. The things that are tedious, often needing repetition, so minute most people never give any recognition for them getting done. Who really likes to do those kinds of things?

But, listen! God says it is when one is *faithful* in doing the little things, that person will be *faithful* in the *big* things, or *many* things. Now that is what makes God's Heart joyous. That is the essence of God. *Faithful* in the *least*, *faithful* in the *much*. Aren't you glad God is *faithful* in the *least* in your life?

Think about this for a minute. Think about the practical little things in life. For instance, taking care of ourselves physically...getting the proper amount of sleep, rest, nourishment, hydration. For instance, getting an education from Kindergarten through High School...perhaps college, maybe further. For instance, getting a job and making a living. For instance, getting married and having kids...keeping the heritage of our family intact. For instance, thinking ahead for the years of retirement, not wasting all the funds God channels through our hands in our lifetime...including looking to see Proverbs 13:22 (*a good man leaveth an inheritance to his children's children*). For instance...well, you make a list of all the *practical little things* in life. The *Life of Christ* IN US desires to be found *pistos* in ALL these things! It is His Nature. It is Him.

And, then, He desires to show us just how *much* He will bring our way. Faithful. Dependable. In all things trustworthy. If we *abandon to Christ* in ALL things, especially the *least/little* things, He will bring the *much* to our lives. Well, amen.

Living Life as a faithful Christian is all about allowing the Grace of God to Live through us.

Chapter 48

Grow In Grace

> But grow in grace, and in the knowledge
> of our Lord and Savior Jesus Christ.
> 2 Peter 3:18

It is very interesting to know that Peter opened his epistle with a similar statement:
> Grace and peace be multiplied unto you through the knowledge of God, and of Jesus our Lord. 2 Peter 1:2

Everywhere we look in the NT the writers are wanting us to have *much grace*. They say that in their salutations. They say that in their texts. They say that in their closings. *Grace, grace, God's grace…amen.*

I dare not explain *what* God's grace is, without taking time also to explain *why* multitudes of Christians are not enjoying His Grace, or not recognizing *what* it is if they do. However, in my estimation, this *why* is the result of erroneous definitions of *what* the *grace of God* is in the first place. That is one reason I have chosen 2 Peter 3:18 as the text verse for this important chapter.

Holy Spirit through Peter has penned a significant *do* for Believers. And yet, this being *parabolic* does not give us the final word on the subject. It is a beginning, for me, when I give what I see Scripture defining and describing as the *grace of God*.

But, first let me give you the most common erroneous, or incomplete at the least, definition scholars have given for the *grace of God:* God's *unmerited favor.* That's a real nebulous thought, isn't it? I ask a couple of questions to make myself more definitive and clear…

> Can you name me anything we are given from God that is NOT *God's unmerited favor? Anything?*
> Can you tell me how anyone can *grow* (that's what Peter has said we are to *do*) in God's *unmerited favor? Grow?*

Sounds like something we are to *do* to get something that is *unmerited,* according to the previous definition. By default, an oxymoron.

So, the answers to these two questions led me to a concordance to look at *every* verse in Scripture where the word *grace* appears. A lengthy task. *Grace* appears 170 times total in the Bible. 39 times in the Old Testament. 131 times in the New Testament.

I have been interested in this word *grace* for many years. Actually, since I was first Born Again. It is *what* worked to bring about my New Birth.

For by grace are ye saved... Ephesians 2:8

So, I was given the *unmerited favor* of God, but others are not? God liked me more than others? I don't think so. That led me to start thinking that *grace* might involve the *unmerited favor* of God, but it had to include more. What was that more? And each verse kept leading to one thing, actually one Person: the LORD. He is clearly *involved* in *grace* in so many verses in Scripture.

By whom *(Jesus)* we have received *grace*... Romans 1:5

Being justified freely by His *(God) grace* through the redemption that is in Christ Jesus... Romans 3:24

Therefore being justified by faith, we have peace with God through our Lord Jesus Christ: By whom *(Jesus)* also we have access by faith into this *grace* wherein we stand... Romans 5:1-2

And He *(Jesus)* said unto me, My *(Jesus) grace* is sufficient for thee: for My *(Jesus)* strength is made perfect in weakness... 2 Corinthians 12:9

These verses (just a smidgeon of the multitude) show the *work/grace* that God does for Saints.

Scripture equates *grace* and *truth* with Jesus Christ:

And the Word was made flesh, and dwelt among us, and we beheld His glory, the glory as of the only begotten of the Father, full of *grace* and *truth*. John 1:14

And of His fullness have all we received, and *grace* for *grace*. John 1:16

For the law was given by Moses, but *grace* and *truth* came by Jesus Christ. John 1:17

Listen to a couple of explanations that add clarity to all this.

> "Grace is not simply leniency when we have sinned. Grace is the *enabling gift of God not to sin*. Grace is *power*, not just pardon." John Piper

Whose power is that? Jesus'.

> "Grace is but *Glory* begun, and *Glory* is but Grace perfected." Jonathan Edwards

Whose glory? Jesus'. Grace, power, glory. All in Jesus Christ. All a gift working in us.

Now listen. The answer to the *what* is simply *the unmerited favor of everything God DOES for us*. It is *His* DOING that IS His *grace*. His doing is an *unmerited favor* of God toward us. There is no working of the *unmerited favor* of God without someone *doing something!* And something that only God can do.

This is the *why* (the reason) so many Believers are not knowing or recognizing, and receiving the *what* of the *grace/working* of God in their lives. Instead of looking for the *grace/working* of God in their lives, too many Christians are launching out trying to *do* what only God can do!

Q – How does *grace* work for you? It always involves something God *does*. Make your own list.

So, Peter's verse tells us to grow in the *workings* of Christ through us, and to grow in the *knowledge/know experientially* (Gr. *gnosis*) of our Lord and Savior Jesus Christ. *Gnosis* is talking about *present and fragmentary knowledge* as contrasted with *epignosis, clear and exact knowledge* which expresses a more thorough participation in the object of knowledge on the part of the subject. Without a doubt this growth was important for Peter to mention as was the growth in *grace*.

Therefore, before we finish the chapter, let me mention this: one of the best ways to *grow* in the *knowledge* of our Lord Jesus Christ is to spend much time in *His Mind*. This is the only Mind that can reveal the things of the Spirit of God, for they are Spiritually discerned. Any Saint spending time in the *natural mind* is not only wasting his time, but thinking with the mind that Scripture tells us receives nothing from the Spirit of God.

Time in the *Mind of Christ* leads to a growth in the knowledge of Him. Period. Reading Scripture in His Mind gives this growth. Listening to teaching and preaching in His Mind gives this growth. Any meditation on Truth gives this growth. *Growth in the knowledge of our Lord Jesus Christ* can come only from time in *His Mind*.

Q – How much time do you spend in *His Mind*?

We can grow in the *what*, His *grace,* by spending time in *His Mind*. We grow in the *knowledge* of Him by spending time in *His Mind*.

There is one more consideration before we close this chapter. It is the word *grow*. We have seen it many times so far, but did you know that the Greek word translated *grow* is *auxano?* It means to grow up, to increase, to enlarge. And it is used only four (4) times in the NT of something that Saints are to *grow into*. Wow. In addition to our text, here are the other three:

> But speaking the truth in love, may *grow* up into *Him* in all things, which is the head, even Christ. Ephesians 4:15
> As newborn babes, desire the sincere milk of the *word*, that ye may *grow* thereby: if so be ye have tasted that the Lord is *gracious*. 1 Peter 2:2-3
> We are bound to thank God always for you, brethren, as it is meet, because that your *faith groweth* exceedingly...2 Thessalonians 1:3

Interesting. Our Lord Jesus Christ is at the center of each. Him. The word (Him). Faith (His Faith). Along with His grace and the knowledge of Him as Peter has said in our text.

More about Jesus would I know, More of His grace to others show...always more of Jesus Christ.
More of His saving fullness see, More of His love who died for me....always more of Jesus Christ.

Thank You, Lord Jesus, that we CAN know You, and that we CAN grow to have more of Your grace.

Chapter 49

The Fear of the LORD

> The fear of the LORD is the beginning of knowledge:
> but fools despise wisdom and instruction.
> Proverbs 1:7

Fear, in our text, is NOT *to be afraid of, to cow down scared.* Why would any Saint of God who has the Almighty, Omniscient, Omnipotent, Omnipresent LORD AS OUR LIFE (*His Life IS our Life*) be afraid of His Life? Incredibly false teaching has yielded a cowardice of the Saints facing life as if God is mean, vindictive, and lurking behind every corner waiting to punish every little mistake. And, keeping a list of all mistakes for further retribution AND, keeping all gifts at bay from His *pitiful bunch.*

Before we go any further, let me give you a clear example of how false those ideas are.

> If any of you lack wisdom, let him ask of God, that giveth to all men liberally, and upbraideth not; and it shall be given him. But let him ask in faith, nothing wavering, For he that wavereth is like a wave of the sea driven with the wind and tossed. For let not that man think that he shall receive any thing of the Lord. A double-minded man is unstable in all his ways. James 1:5-8

There is much in these four verses, but suffice it for now to focus only on one thought: God makes no mention here, in the previous 4 verses, nor in the following 3 verses, of anything about His keeping at bay His wisdom until *any of us* have straightened up *our* life, done so much penance, or done so many *good* things that *we* are now *worthy* of being *given* His wisdom. Wow.

Actually, the one thing God does mention about our *doing* is for us to not float back-and-forth from *His Mind* in us to the *natural mind* still in us. Make note of something important that Scripture teaches: only Christians have 2 minds. Only Christians can be *double-minded*. Granted, the *natural mind* does have two *sides* to it (from *the tree of the knowledge of good and evil*), but the *natural mind* (the mind of Unbelievers) is still just *one* mind.

It is of huge importance to know that the Greek for *double-minded* is *dipsuchos,* from *dis* (twice) and *psuche* (soul, mind). Double-souled or double-minded. The mind is in the soul. This lends itself to the explanation given in the previous paragraph along with the admonition over and over we have seen for the Christian to Live in the Soul of Christ and not the *old soul.*

Now listen, the Hebrew word for the English *fear* in Proverbs 1:7 is *yirah*. Its source is *yare*. All the mentions of *yare* and *yirah* are connected to different forms of mentioning God. *Fear of the* LORD or *fear of GOD,* in one form or another, are mentioned over 500 times in the Old Testament. The meaning is very special. It tells of God speaking to His people to *truly recognize God as all-powerful, worship God,* and/or to *recognize God in reverence and awe*. It is not a direct command for motivation effecting godly living, but rather to be a devotee or follower.

Here is something incredible, I think: *fear* appears 114 times in the New Testament, yet only a handful as *fear of the Lord* or *fear of God* in one form or another. Why the minimal number of times in NT times (which is for us today)? The only answer has to be the New Creation that Believers are, the indwelling of Holy Spirit as our Life, and the fellowship that is different for us than for OT Children of God.

The admonition to Believers today is to *truly recognize God as all-powerful, worship God,* and/or to *recognize God in reverence and awe,* just as in OT days but with Holy Spirit being the One to Live it through NT Saints' earthsuits. The Greek *phobos* carries with it the capability of a good connotation. Look at two great examples from two different writers Holy Spirit spoke through:

> Then had the churches rest throughout all Judea and Galilee and Samaria, and were edified; and walking in the fear of the Lord, and in the comfort of the Holy Ghost, were multiplied. Acts 9:31

Submitting yourselves one to another in the fear of God.
Ephesians 5:21

So what is *the fear of the Lord* today? The *fear of the Lord* is not the END...it is the BEGINNING. It leads to the beginning of *knowledge* just as Solomon wrote. It is the beginning of *wisdom* as Solomon wrote (Proverbs 9:10 – note the difference between knowledge and wisdom, see chapter 10). It is a fountain of life as Solomon wrote (Proverbs 14:27). But we must assume Solomon did not know what lay ahead for God's children. It leads to Colossians 1:27 and 3:1-4, and John 15:13-15. So, notice all that the *fear of the Lord* brings us to today:

The fear of the LORD is the beginning of knowledge...
Proverbs 1:7

The fear of the LORD is the beginning of wisdom: and the knowledge of the holy is understanding. Proverbs 9:10

In the fear of the LORD is strong confidence: and His children shall have a place of refuge. Proverbs 14:26

The fear of the LORD is a fountain of life... Proverbs 14:27

Even the mystery which hath been hid from ages and from generations, but now is made manifest to His saints: To whom God would make known what is the riches of the glory of this mystery among the Gentiles; which is *Christ in you, the hope of glory.*
Colossians 1:26-27 (italics my emphasis)

If ye then be risen with Christ, seek those things which are above, where Christ sitteth on the right hand of God. Set your affections on things above, not on things on the earth. For ye are dead, and your life is hid with Christ in God. When Christ, who is our life, shall appear, then shall ye also appear with Him in glory.
Colossians 3:1-4

Greater love hath no man than this, that a man lay down his life for his friends. Ye are My friends, if ye do whatsoever I command you. Henceforth I call you not servants; for the servant knoweth not what his lord

doeth: but I have called you friends; for all things that I have heard of my Father I have made known unto you.
John 15:13-15

Let me mention again the beautiful description given by Kenneth Boa and Gail Burnett, "the fear of the LORD is the heart-stopping realization of the glory, majesty, and power of God and of His right to absolute sovereignty over His creation. Without this realization, none of us will ever fall on our face before the Almighty."

Keep in mind any parabolism, and enjoy the Spiritual Truth. Those who have His Spiritual eyes, His Spiritual ears, and His Spiritual Mind will rejoice in their *fear of the Lord*. It is the recognition, admiration, and appropriation of just Who God is…and, an appreciation that HE IS OUR GOD.

All of this should lead us to desire to experience His Life to be Our Life every moment of every day.

Chapter 50

His Work...His Will

*For it is God which worketh in you both
to will and to do of His good pleasure.
Philippians 2:13*

One important Spiritual Truth needs to be mentioned clearly again (I have said so in varying ways throughout the book): the *will* of God mentioned here is the Greek word *thelo*. It is a word that embodies *deciding on a plan AND pressing on to carry out the plan*. It is not *the* plan itself. All plans that end up being carried out originate in one of our *hearts*, which is the culmination of the work of the mind, the emotions, and the decision-maker (will) we choose, functioning in a unified manner. Here Holy Spirit tells us through the Apostle Paul that God is working to carry out a plan He has prepared and decided to bring to fruition in us. It is of *His good pleasure*, to the benefit of God's will and gracious purpose.

In a very stirring story in Genesis ch.28, God placed NO CONDITIONS ON Jacob when He said to him: "...I will not leave thee, until I have done that which I have spoken to thee of" Genesis 28:15.

> I am the LORD God of Abraham thy father, and the God of Isaac: the land whereon thou liest, to thee I will give it, and to thy seed; And thy seed shall be as the dust of the earth; and thou shalt spread abroad to the west, and to the east, and to the north, and to the south: and in thee and in thy seed shall all the families of the earth be blessed. And behold, I am with thee, and will keep thee in all places whither thou goest, and will bring thee again into this land; for I will not leave thee, until I have done that which I have spoken to thee of. Genesis 28:13-15.

God has given you and me a promise today. He has told us in Hebrews 13:5, "I will never leave thee, nor forsake thee." His words in Philippians 1:6 (ch.52) tie into Hebrews 13:5 to give us part of the same promise God gave Jacob in Genesis 28. (note: some Old Testament promises were for specific people at specific times, as with Jacob in Genesis 28, and not for any others, BUT…God has given part of the same promise to us Saints in the New Testament)

We can live our lives **knowing** God is with us wherever we are. And not only that, He is carrying out the plan He has for us. God has promised throughout His love letter to His children that He has not only *begun* a good work in us, but *will perform it* until Jesus comes. It is His will to work it through to completion. And it will please Him. Well, amen!

Jacob didn't have to *perform* anything in any way in order to know that God was going to complete what He started. God will always complete that which He has begun. He does it for His own glory. He does it for us, for our eternal blessing. We are not what we have made ourselves to be, but we are, and will be, what God has made, and is making, us to be. That is the Grace of God. That is His work in our lives.

With God's promise in Hebrews 13:5, God adds that not only will He not leave us (He will be with us), but He will never forsake (abandon) us. (see also 13:8). So, remember, it could be an impertinence to say ourselves, "If God is with us…" Or, "If God will show up…"

A couple of words of *warning*:
- never doubt that God is in control of your life
- never worry that God cannot worketh out what He has started
- never question that God will not perform what is His responsibility
- never *claim* or *stand* on verses that are not for everyone

As Barbara and I look back over our lives, we can testify that God has worked out His plan for us every year. We have been places we never dreamed we would go. We have done things we seldom ever knew we would ahead of time. But in each place, in each day/week/month/year, God has been there guiding us along the path He had planned for our lives.

So, keep in mind: God has a plan for your life. God is constantly at work, working out His plan for you. He is in your choices you make each day…just go ahead and make the choices that are in your Heart (His Heart in you!). God will see to it that His plan is worked out. You and I cannot *get out of God's will for us.*

Enjoy knowing that God has good pleasure in directing the steps of your Life.

Chapter 51

All Things Working Together

And we know that all things work together for good to them that love God, to them who are the called according to his purpose.
Romans 8:28

 This verse does not say, *all things work out*, or *all things work together for good*, as so many quote it, or say it says. It says, "And we know that all things work together for good **to them that love God, to them who are the called according to His purpose.**" This is a huge difference just in that it is ONLY Christians who can *Love God*. Then there is a great difference in that God tells us that those who *love Him* are ONLY those who have first experienced His Love. And it is ONLY those with the Love of God in them, which is the Love that Loves God. All this is the essence of John 3:16...

  For God so loved the world that He gave His only
  begotten Son, that whosoever believeth in Him should
  not perish, but have everlasting life.

...and the essence of 1 John 4:19...

  We love Him, because He first loved us.

Wow! Soak on those two verses for a minute in relation to Romans 8:28. So, what say ye about all the things going on in your life, and those things to come???

 It may not surprise you to find that this may be the shortest chapter in this book, but it is still one of the most important. First of all, the Truth herein means you should NEVER let any anxiety be present in your life. God IS in control of your situations and circumstances. Second, He will not let anything happen without it first passing through His hands.

Third, the typical way we think something is *good* (moral goodness) or *bad/evil* (wicked, moral deficiency) is from the *natural mind*, from the *tree of the knowledge of good and evil*. Either way that mind leads us to *death*, sometimes physical but mostly spiritual. That is the wrong mind for us to be thinking with. From the *Mind of Christ* we will see things as He sees them...Life. His Mind takes us to His Life. What is His Life in each issue we face? Romans 8:28. And here the word *good* is a Greek word meaning *for our benefit*. Well, amen.

The Love of God in every Believer works all things together for something useful and profitable, beneficial, to those who love God and are the called according to His purpose.

Chapter 52

God Will Complete What He Started

*Being confident of this very thing,
that He which hath begun a good work in you
will perform it until the day of Jesus Christ.*
Philippians 1:6

This is an astounding Truth! It is actually two Truths.
1. God is the One who started this *good* work in us
2. God WILL *perform/complete* what He started

...all this before He takes us Home.

Wow! That is pretty spectacular, isn't it? What a great chapter to complete this first volume with.

So, let's look at these two things in more detail. *Being confident of this very thing, that He which hath begun a good work in you...* At our New Birth, becoming a New Creation (remember 2 Corinthians 5:17 – chapter 7), God initiated and established our Eternal Life. He put His Life (Eternal Life) *in us* as *our* Life. We NOW have Eternal Life. We do not have to wait until we die physically to *get, be given,* or in any other way *possess* Eternal Life. He is our Eternal Life NOW. That's a pretty good start of a *good work*, don't you believe?!? Along with placing Eternal Life *in us*, God gave us all the benefits of His indwelling. We have talked about them all through this book. Holy Spirit, with the pens of the Apostles Paul, Peter, and John along with James, half-brother of the Lord Jesus, has told us so many things that are a part of the *good work* begun *in us* by God.

Let me point out (remind us of) something very interesting, but also very important: anytime we see the word *create, created,* or *creation* we must keep in mind that God is the ONLY One Who can *create*, make something out of nothing. Let us look at a verse that shows us something God did at the start AS we were Born Again. Ephesians 2:8-10...

> For by grace are ye saved through faith; and that not of yourselves: it is the gift of God: Not of works, lest any man should boast. For we are His workmanship, created in Christ Jesus unto good works, which God hath before ordained that we should walk in them.

This life here on earth for a Christian (from the New Birth) is about *walking in the good works* God has ordained and *created into* us.

Grace is the work of God. He is how we are Born Again. His Faith *cemented* our believing God's record of His Son. Since salvation is, and can only be, by His Grace, it cannot be of ourselves. It is *the* gift of God. Not *a* gift, but *the* gift. It is special, not just *any* gift. It is the Lord Jesus Christ Himself!

Salvation is not of *works* because it cannot be of us, it cannot be earned, it cannot be payment for something we have done, it cannot be something that might lead us to our boasting of our accomplishing/gaining/etc. Romans 11:6 tells us the same thing...

> And if by grace, then it is no more of works: otherwise grace is no more grace. But if it be of works, then it is no more grace: otherwise work is no more work.

Now, God then tells us *we are His workmanship*. He did the work in our salvation. AND, in our New Birth He *created* us *in Christ Jesus unto good works* (a part of our being *in Christ*). Then is when He started this *good work* in us.

OK, we now can look at *being confident of this very thing, that He...will perform it until the day of Jesus Christ*. WOW! Here is a special writing from Holy Spirit telling us once more that all that goes on in our earthsuit from our day of salvation is a *good work* that GOD WILL PERFORM. God will perform. Not us. Not us performing. Not us under any law of performance. God will perform. And He will do so *until the day of Jesus Christ*. The *day of Jesus Christ* is the Lord's return for His Saints. We can live our lives *knowing* God is with us wherever we are. And not only that, He is carrying out His plan in His Heart that He has for us. God has promised throughout His Love letter to His children that He has not only *begun* a good work in us, but *will perform it* until Jesus comes. It is

His *Will/Heart* to work it through to completion. And it will please Him. Well, amen!

Confidence that God began a good work in us at our New Birth and will work it through to completion (it is His doing), creates in us His peace, His joy, His comfort, His rest, His security. Well, amen.

Scriptural References

Genesis
- Ch. 1 & 2 — 114
- 1:31 — 32
- 3:1 — 20
- 15:6 — 57
- Ch. 28 — 166,167
- 28:13-15 — 166

Exodus
- 20:12 — 58

Leviticus
- 19:32 — 58

Numbers
- 13:2 — 56
- 13:30 — 56

Deuteronomy
- 4:10 — 58

1 Kings
- 12:6 — 58

Job
- 32:4 — 58

Psalm
- 18:2 — 90
- Ch. 23 — 83,128,142
- 23:1 — 131
- 46:1 — 90
- 78:2 — 23
- 91:2 — 90
- 119:165 — 144,145

Proverbs
- 1:1-7 — 48
- 1:5 — 47
- 1:7 — 48,162,163,164
- 3:5-6 — 73
- 3:7-8 — 74
- 4:23 — 50
- 9:10 — 164
- 12:25 — 146
- 13:22 — 157
- 14:26 — 164
- 14:27 — 164

Isaiah
- 26:3 — 138,144,147

Matthew
- 6:24-25 — 151
- 6:30 — 151
- 6:31-34 — 151
- Ch. 13 — 23,52,54
- 13:10-11 — 22
- 13:11 — 52
- 13:12-17 — 22
- 13:34-35 — 23,54
- 17:2 — 109
- 21:13 — 125
- 23:1-3,5 — 100

Mark
- Ch. 4 — 23
- 4:1-2 — 23
- 4:9-12 — 23
- 4:33-34 — 24
- 9:2 — 109

Luke
- 2:19 — 51
- 16:10 — 156

John
- Ch. 1 — 99
- 1:1 — 75,81
- 1:4 — 75
- 1:11 — 61,105
- 1:11-12 — 105,178
- 1:12 — 60,61
- 1:14 — 159
- 1:16,17 — 159
- 3:3,6-7 — 178
- 3:7,1-7 — 27
- 3:16 — 169
- 5:24 — 87

5:39-40	75	4:3	57,99
Ch. 6	19	4:4	99
6:29	58	5:1-2	159
6:63	17,75	Ch. 6	33,41
8:32,36	87,133	6:6	87
8:36	87	6:2,11	87
Ch. 10	83,128	Ch. 7	33,41
10:1-10	129	7:23	33
10:10	42,79,80	7:24-25	33
10:11	128	Ch. 8	33,41
10:22-27	147	8:1	87,134,147
11:25-26	78	8:2	87
12:15	90	8:7	43
Ch. 14	138	8:9-11	88
14:6	81,90,178	8:9,16	30,80
14:12	115,119	8:11	80,111,112,115
14:26	26	8:13-17	111
14:27	90,135,138	8:17	79,87
Ch. 15	83,118	8:28	147,169,170
15:1-5	83	10:8-17	28,71
15:5	83,89,118	10:9-10	40
15:9-10	90	10:17	70
15:11	90	11:6	172
15:13-15	164,165	12:1	108
20:27-29	59	12:1-2	107
Acts		15:7	88
1:13	24	**1 Corinthians**	
Ch. 2	50	1:2	87
2:1-4	24	1:30	88,90
9:1-2	82	2:14	18,41,43,53
9:31	163	2:16	43
11:25-26	82	6:19	87
16:31	56	14:33	41
Romans		15:10	90
Ch. 1	58	**2 Corinthians**	
1:5	159	2:14	87
1:6-7	87	4:3-4	71
1:21-22,24	58	5:17	34,87,171
1:26,28	58	5:21	87
1:17	154	12:9	141.159
3:24	87,159		

Galatians
2:4	87
2:20	68,81,88,108
3:6	57
3:6-7	87
3:8-9	87
3:24-25	87
4:7	87
Ch. 5	145
5:1	87,134
5:13	87
5:22	63,66,68,90
5:22-23	45,123,126

Ephesians
Ch. 1	33
1:3	85,88,120
1:4-14	86
1:4	87
1:6	88
1:7	87,108
1:13	88
1:14	90
2:5	87,88
2:6	87
2:8	159
2:8-10	172
2:10	87,90
2:18	86,88
3:6	87
3:8-16	118
3:9	23
3:12	88
3:14-21	87
3:15	87
3:17-19	96
3:20-21	114
4:15	161
4:22-32	103
4:24	102
5:8	87
5:18	51,97
5:21	164
5:30	87
6:10	87

Philippians
1:6	167,171
1:27	103
2:10-11	62
2:13	90,166
3:19	80
4:4	146,147
4:6-9	143,146,147
4:7	88
4:8	140
4:9	58
4:11	141,142
4:12	142
4:13	87,90,117
4:19	88,142, 147,149

Colossians
1:19	93
1:26	23,164
1:27	33,89,155, 164
2:6	80
2:6-8	94
2:9-10	93
2:10	88
2:12-13	88
3:1-4	80,90,164
3:3	88
3:4	77,108

1 Thessalonians
5:23	35
5:24	90

2 Thessalonians
1:3   161
1 Timothy
2:6   87
6:6-8   141,143
2 Timothy
1:7   90,126,147
2:1-2   154
2:24   124
3:14-17   15
3:16   18
Hebrews
2:10   90
2:14-15   90
9:14   87
11:1   63
11:6   66
13:5   143,167
1 Peter
1:15-16   178
1:18-19   87
1:23   28,87
2:2-3   161
5:5   58
5:7   147
2 Peter
1:2   158
1:3-4   28
1:4   90
1:5-8   125
1:5-11   30
3:18   105,158
James
1:5-8   147,162
1:22   51
2:23   57
3:13   48
3:17   45

1 John
1:1   75
1:9   147
2:12   87
2:15-16   141
4:1   121
4:19   97,169
5:10-12,13   28
5:12   29,30,81
5:13   29,90
5:18   88

On Being Born Again

Our Lord Jesus Christ made some very definitive statements about becoming a Christian and *receiving* Eternal Life. Read these verses carefully and my further comments, and then if you need further explanation or answers to some questions please contact me or someone you know who can give you God's wisdom and answers:

> Jesus saith unto him, I am the way, the truth, and the life: no man cometh unto the Father, but by Me. John 14:6
> Jesus answered and said unto him, Verily, verily, I say unto thee, Except a man be born again, he cannot see the kingdom of God…That which is born of the flesh is flesh; and that which is born of the Spirit is spirit. Marvel not that I said unto thee, Ye must be born again. John 3:3, 6-7
> He came unto His own, and His own received Him not. But as many as received Him, to them gave He power to become the sons of God, even to them that believe on His name. John 1:11-12

Within these words are the *way* of salvation. Many other scriptures lead the way to Eternal Life (Jesus) also. Everyone will die the physical death, and then face the judgment of God.

Some people call this salvation being *saved*. There is truth in that, but I like to make it plain, clear, and complete that a New Birth better describes becoming a Christian and *knowing* you have become one.

Basically, anyone who has not been *Born Again* thinks the way to Heaven is a path of *good works*. However, God's standard is perfection. Jesus Himself was perfect. And God says:

> But as He which hath called you is holy, so be ye holy in all manner of conversation (behavior); Because it is written, Be ye holy; for I am holy. 1 Peter 1:15-16

Are you perfect? Are you holy? Do you live up to that? Well, we all know the truth is that a sinner living a perfect life is impossible. But God sent

His perfect Son to be the perfect substitutionary, all-sufficient atoning sacrifice for all sinners' sin at His Cross of Calvary. Full forgiveness of one's sin can only come through a sinner confessing their sin, asking God for His forgiveness, receiving His grace (His payment) by trusting in the Lord Jesus Christ and His death and shedding of His blood for that perfect sacrifice for one's sin.

Good works do matter for a Christian, but only after salvation, not to escape God's righteous judgment.

Is there a perfect prayer to pray for God's forgiveness? Perhaps. But God knows a repentant heart and a sinner's desire for His forgiveness. And, there are many Scriptures that give direction as to a *righteous* prayer for asking God's forgiveness. The following will help you if that is your desire:

> *Dear Lord Jesus Christ, I thank You for dying upon Your Cross for me, a guilty sinner, paying the penalty for my sin. I ask You, Lord Jesus, to have mercy on me. I believe and trust You are the Way, the Truth, and the Life. And there is no other. I trust your payment for my sin, and accept, and receive You gladly, as my Savior.*
>
> *Thank You for cleansing me and forgiving me of all my sin – past, present, and future. I believe, and by Your Holy Spirit now Living in me, KNOW I am redeemed, and You will never leave me nor forsake me. You are Christ my Savior, my Lord, my God, my Life – forever! Amen.*

Just as you are *Born Again* by God's grace when you trust in the Lord Jesus Christ and His payment, you are kept by God's grace for all eternity. Enjoy God's mercy, His love, His grace for all eternity as a *Born Again* child of God, one who WAS a sinner but is NOW an HOLY Saint.

books by

B. Lee McDowell

Dowadad Press, Publisher
A division of Lee McDowell Christian Ministries, Inc.
P. O. Box 633244, Nacogdoches, TX, 75963

Books In Print

Seagulls Don't Lie!
    The Truth shall MAKE you free!

God's Words Bring *Life*
    Christ's Life becoming your Life

Books To Come

The Images of God & Man
    the trichotomies in diagrams

all i want is Jesus! – Vol. 1
    His Love, His Grace, His Sound Mind, His Shepherding

all i want is Jesus! – Vol. 2
    His Faith, His Hope, His Joy, His Peace, His Acceptance, His Presence, His Mercy

Living In Christ's Pasture
 a LIFE of peace, protection, and plenitude

Growing in God's Grace
 MUCH more than the mysterious "unmerited favor"

The Math of Life
 Experiencing the Life of Christ in your personal finances

B. Lee McDowell
Lee McDowell Christian Ministries
P.O. Box 633244, Nacogdoches, Texas 75963
936-645-9091
leemccm.wixsite.com/lmcm

B. Lee McDowell
About the Author

Born into a family of educators, B. Lee McDowell instead set his sights on other fields and first became a professional golfer before settling into a lucrative sales career. But God had different plans.

With a father who was a college tennis player and later a multi-sport coach, Lee was involved in athletics from an early age. An injury at age 12 changed his athletic plans, and he turned to golf, playing on the Texas A&M University Golf Team, ultimately winning the Texas State Amateur Golf Championship, and playing on the PGA Tour for a couple of years.

In his late twenties, he became a salesman, where he worked his way up to become a manager/vice-president of the world's largest small boat dealership, Louis DelHomme Marine in Houston, Texas.

But in 1981, God called Lee to a life of ministry. He studied at Southwestern Baptist Theological Seminary, and began his life's calling. Having been a minister in various forms in various towns for over 35 years, his extensive experiences and acquaintances have given him a broad perspective of Life as a Christian which show forth in his writings.

Life changed in 2003 when Lee suffered a major heart attack. God then had him serving in part-time pastoral roles until his 70th birthday. At that point, God moved Lee into writing books and blogs, and doing discipleship training and counseling. And from an encounter 20 years before at a men's retreat where he got the idea of doing ministry at a local park on Sunday mornings, Lee has been leading the ministry, *Christ in the Park*, at Festival Park in Nacogdoches for over 4 years now.

B. Lee McDowell is the president of Lee McDowell Christian Ministries, a preaching, teaching, discipleship-making ministry.

Lee and his wife of 52 years, Barbara, have 2 children and four grandchildren.

B. Lee McDowell
Lee McDowell Christian Ministries
P. O. Box 633244, Nacogdoches, TX 75963
936-645-9091
www.leemccm.wixsite.com/lmcm